The Wolves of Mars

The Wolves of Mars

*An Introductory History of Rome
from the Rise of the Monarchy to
the Fall of the Western Empire*

Aeon History

uxori liberisque

and

fratri parentibusque

Contents

Introduction

If Twitter (or X, as it's called these days) had existed during the fall of the Roman Empire, #RomeIsFalling would probably have trended. But behind this mighty collapse was a centuries-old saga of ambition, intrigue, and innovation that laid the foundation for every empire that followed. Unlike the trending topics of modern social media, the destiny of the Roman Empire didn't vanish within a few hours. As it is said, "Rome wasn't built in a day," and it certainly didn't disappear in a flash. Dive deep into the chronicles of Rome, and you might just see reflections of our world today.

The Roman Empire wasn't the first in human history, and it wasn't even the largest. However, it had certain features that made it unique, and its legacy is enduring and influential in the contemporary world, far beyond its old boundaries. While empires like the Mongols or the British had larger territories, the Roman Empire's longevity was unmatched. For over two millennia, its institutions and laws have directly influenced a large portion of the modern world, including foundational aspects of legal systems in places ranging from the UK to parts of Africa (Kinder & Hilgemann, 1996).

Rome in Modern Culture

Rome has captivated people's attention for ages. The stories of the Romans reflect their virtues and glory but also highlight their vices and weaknesses. Films, media, and pop culture have taken popular figures from ancient Rome to depict controversial (therefore attractive) aspects of the Romans' lives. Yet, most of these modern interpretations are guided by marketing rules rather than historical rigor. The attempt to move the audience seems to be more important than a reliable academic background. This type of content plays a valuable role in introducing people to historical knowledge, but it is usually fraught with errors that lead to misconceptions.

For history enthusiasts, it is a great challenge to find resources that can balance reliable and relevant information with an engaging storyline. History is a colossal collection of facts, battles, important figures, and processes that are hard to digest for those who aren't used to academic works. But those who don't belong to the academic world shouldn't need to suffer through those heavy-reading books of many volumes to unravel the most interesting secrets of our history. They need to find some better-researched sources to learn about our past than a series from a streaming service. That should be left as a means of entertainment and perhaps a way to foster our curiosity to learn the truth behind the artificial modern plots.

The past is always a source of endless intrigue. What is true and what is not about the good (or bad) old days? Have we left savage practices behind, or do we still resemble our ancestors from over 2500 years ago? Is humankind really moving forward to a promising future? These are the types of questions that move us to learn history. We want to understand the past to explain our present. But over 2500 years of history encompass too many topics to delve into. Almost 2,000 years of Roman history seem unfathomable. How can we discriminate between the "need to know" and the "nice to know"?

The Purpose of This Book

This book aims to zoom in on the prominent figures, milestones, and fundamental processes that marked the evolution of the history of Rome and elucidate how our Western civilization developed out of its rich legacy. However, this doesn't mean that the understanding of Roman history and its long-lasting

heritage is restricted by a Eurocentric scope. On the
contrary, it aims to broaden the scope and provide
insightful explanations of how different cultures were
blended throughout history, making today's world
what it is. The Romans interacted in many different
ways with neighboring cultures and learned from
other civilizations, and their influence persists in
present-day cultures all over the world.

By reading this book, you will not only gain
knowledge but also a newfound appreciation for the
monumental influence of the Roman Empire on the
modern world (*Traces of Ancient Rome in the
Modern World*, n.d.). New perspectives on the
distant past that lies beneath the ground of our
modern culture are at the core of this book. It's a
comprehensive guide to a fascinating past that
shaped our mindset and values. The framework for
understanding the empire laid the foundation of a
timeless ideal: one nation, one power. Somehow, it
still summarizes the current objectives of order,
peace, stability, and progress.

To facilitate comprehension of the long and
complex evolution of Roman civilization, the book is
organized into three parts that condense major
periods: The Monarchy (753–509 B.C.E.), The
Republic (509–27 B.C.E.), and The Roman Empire
(27 B.C.E.– 476 C.E.). The first part covers
prehistoric Italy, including the primitive peoples who
lived on the peninsula, the mythical beginnings of
ancient Rome, and the first political organization: the
Roman Monarchy.

The second part covers the Roman Republic. The political and social organization of this period not only laid the foundation for the greatest empire of antiquity but also formed the basis of Western political and legal structures down to the present.

The third and last part is dedicated to exploring and explaining the details of the Roman Empire, beginning with the progressive concentration of power in the figure of Augustus until its final collapse (at least in the West).

It is impossible to understand Rome without considering the interplay between politics, culture, military conquests, and social dynamics. Each part is divided into chapters that explain the evolution of social, economic, and political changes in a chronological format to simplify the complex progression of Rome for a non-specialist reader. Instead of slogging through multiple academic texts, this book provides an integrated insight, alternating relevant details with a depiction of the big picture.

The approach to analyzing this evolution is not a mere collection of facts. Instead, *The Wolves of Mars* aims to give a human face to historical events. This version of Rome's history is based on the Romans' stories of ordinary people being part of the legions and attending the amphitheaters, as well as extraordinary leaders like Romulus (if he existed), Scipio, Caesar, Augustus, Marcus Aurelius, and Constantine.

The Enduring Legacy of Rome

Despite the extensive research and coverage dedicated to the ancient Roman era, the subject remains perennially captivating. The following pages retrieve traditional scholarly researchers' main contributions about the period, blended with insights derived from the latest archaeological findings and historical research, ensuring up-to-date and accurate information. In addition to this, the book is a springboard for more in-depth exploration, with curated recommendations for further reading.

The team at Aeon History has a vast appreciation for ancient history and classical archaeology and it believes in the power of history as a tool to shape the present and build a better future. This book is an invitation to discover engaging and accurate insights into a period that seems so distant and, at the same time, is hidden in the little things of the modern world.

Whether you are a history buff who constantly seeks out new books or this is your first approach to studying the past independently, we invite you on a fascinating journey over 2,500 years to vividly revive the days of Roman gladiators, emperors, philosophers, artists, and soldiers. Embark on this adventure of conquests, dominating the *Mare Nostrum* ("Our Sea" – The Mediterranean), fighting against the Barbarians, and building the foundations of Western civilization. *Omnes Salvete!* (Welcome, Everyone!)

Note: All translations from ancient sources are by Aeon History.

Part 1: Prehistoric Italy to the Fall of the Roman Monarchy

(ca. 753 B.C.E. – 509 B.C.E.)

Chapter 1: Italian Prehistory and the Bronze Age

Humans dwelt on the Italian landscape long before Rome existed. Its fertile soil, pleasant climate, and central location ensured that all inhabitants had an opportunity to thrive.

The Geographic Landscape of Prehistoric Italy

Italy is a boot-shaped peninsula measuring 600 miles long and 150 miles wide that juts out into the

Mediterranean basin. It is surrounded by the Adriatic Sea to the east and the Tyrrhenian Sea to the west. The northwest side limits the Ligurian Sea, and the Ionian Sea separates Italy from Greece. Italy also includes two large Mediterranean islands, Sicily and Sardinia.

Italy is crossed from north to south by the Apennine Mountain range, the backbone of the peninsula. While in ancient Greece, mountains served to divide the city-states, or *poleis*, in the Italian Peninsula, the Apennines facilitated trade and connected communities. Italy is enclosed in the north by the highest peaks of Europe, the Alps. At present, they are Italy's natural border with France, Switzerland, Austria, and Slovenia.

Prehistoric Italy didn't have the same political boundaries as in the present, but the native prehistoric people settled in the plains at the bottom of both major mountain ranges. During the last Ice Age, people sheltered in the natural refuges provided by rocky caves on the slopes of the mountains.

Then, after the climate warmed and agricultural knowledge arrived, they searched for lands near the rivers. This process mirrored events in Mesopotamia, along the Tigris and the Euphrates, near the Ganges and Indus Rivers in India, and by the Nile in Egypt. In Italy, the most fertile lands were the basins of key rivers like the Tiber, in central Italy, and the Po, in the north.

The Tiber is the most important river in prehistoric Italy. It is the second longest on the peninsula, behind the Po. The Tiber begins in the Apennine Mountains and runs southwest into the Tyrrhenian Sea. It divides the peninsula into two parts, and it was a source of fresh water for the population that settled in its basin.

Moreover, the river was an important means of transportation that allowed the evolution of trading because of its direct connection with the Mediterranean Sea. It was used to link the peninsula with people from Greece and Northern Africa, like the Phoenicians (*The Geography of Ancient Rome*, n.d.). The river was also a natural frontier, useful in case of attack when the first urban settlements were established in the region.

At a bend in the Tiber River, a system of hills created the perfect landscape to build a city. The hills protected the inhabitants from attack and allowed them to control commerce between the north and south. The weather—hot and dry summers and wet and mild winters—was perfect for animals, crops, and the blossom of a new civilization. It was the perfect place for the Eternal City.

Defining History

Historians have divided the past into periods to facilitate the study and comprehension of humankind's evolution. The concept of "prehistory" refers to everything before the invention of the written word. This is certainly a modern, "Eurocentrist" designation. Even at present, many cultures don't use the written word either to register their present or to study their past, and that definitely doesn't mean they lack a vibrant and meaningful past. Likewise, the so-called "prehistoric" cultures of the ancient world faced the same trials, tribulations, and (often) triumphs of later peoples. Nevertheless, without writing, most of their narrative remains hidden from us.

"History," therefore, starts with the invention of the written word about 6,000 years ago in Mesopotamia. Historians divide it into ages or eras considering relevant events as landmarks that represent the transition from one to another. On the other hand, "prehistory" is divided in regard to the elements human beings mastered to attend to their needs.

About 12,000 years ago, people began to develop techniques for cultivating the land - agriculture. Being able to raise their food allowed and motivated people to settle in river basins. The invention of agriculture marks the beginning of the Neolithic, or New Stone Age. Agriculture and its attendant advancements are often called the Neolithic Revolution.

When people settled and became sedentary, more complex societies emerged. They developed a division of labor and social hierarchies based on the roles people performed or the properties they owned. They learned to cultivate crops, grow livestock, and master metals. Therefore, the Neolithic isn't divided by counting years, but by the stages of humankind's evolution regarding the metals they used to manufacture weapons and tools.

The Deepest Prehistory of Italy

During the Paleolithic and Mesolithic periods (Old and Middle Stone Ages), people lived in nomadic hunter-gatherer tribes. In Italy, the first early human presence can be traced back to 850,000 years ago. According to recent archaeological findings, *Homo erectus* lived 700,000 years ago in the La Pineta district, and it is the oldest human settlement found in Europe. There is also evidence of human presence in the Balzi Rossi caves in Liguria. These were inhabited between 350,000 and 300,000 B.C.E.

The earliest permanent settlements on the peninsula, dating to the Stone Age, belonged to *Homo neanderthalensis* – Neanderthals, who lived in Europe and Southwestern Asia. In Italy, they were at the Saccopastore site by about 250,000 B.C.E.

Homo sapiens sapiens (modern humans) appeared in the region about 34,000 years ago, and their first settlements were found in the Grotta *di Furmane*, Sardinia, Lombardy, and Liguria (Ancos, 2018). Modern humans spread across Europe in the Paleolithic period when a Glacial Era enlarged the polar caps.

While there is still controversy about how or why the Neanderthals disappeared, it is now known that they coexisted with modern humans and even mixed with them. The first modern humans in Europe had dark hair and dark skin, and Neanderthals had red hair. It is believed that the species interacted, and some current modern human populations have genes from both (Carr, 2017), although *Homo sapiens sapiens* predominated.

Archeological remains suggest that the first modern humans who arrived in Italy came from West Asia about 10,000 B.C.E., roughly in the Middle of the Mesolithic period in Europe (Carr, 2017). This was also near the end of the Last Ice Age. Several theories explain the migratory flows. Since they were hunter-gatherers, they probably moved from one place to another, following the animals they hunted for food and their skin and bones. They must have also sought more temperate climates and placed their temporary settlements in places with enough resources, including water and shelter.

During the Last Ice Age, people (Neanderthals and modern humans) sheltered in caves and left paintings on the rocks. The most important remains in Italy are the rock carvings and paintings in Valcamonica. Archeologists have found some remains of that early population, such as stone tools and paintings of animals, probably reflecting what they hunted or part of their rituals to ensure success in the hunt.

Nonetheless, those remains are significantly fewer than at other archaeological sites on the continent, for instance, in France and Spain. This suggests that the region wasn't densely inhabited if compared to other regions of the continent (Carr, 2017).

The Neolithic Revolution in Italy

In Italy, the earliest farmer communities settled between 7,000 and 5,000 B.C.E. (Carr, 2017; Shaw, 2015) in the period called the Neolithic or New Stone Age. These people weren't the same nomadic groups that sheltered in the caves. Instead, it is believed that they came from Greece in boats, sailing along the coasts.

These people had already developed agriculture and sedentary settlements, and the colonization of new lands was due to the depletion of natural resources in their homeland. Colonization processes were a response to social pressure when the distribution of resources wasn't enough to sustain parts of the population.

It doesn't mean that there weren't any native social groups on the peninsula by the time eastern migrants colonized the coastal areas. The central lands of the peninsula were indeed inhabited by the natives, who also developed agriculture and entered the Neolithic period sometime after the arrival of people from Greece and the Balkans.

Even though there were very limited means of communication, prehistoric peoples interacted much more than is usually imagined. They exchanged goods and traded, but, more importantly, they taught and learned from each other. Therefore, agricultural communities inspired hunter-gatherer nomadic groups to introduce new economic and social practices.

One of the key pieces of evidence to prove the passage from nomadic to sedentary life is burial sites. People might have had burial rituals and beliefs regarding the passage from life to death, but burial sites reveal the intention to keep the deceased close by. It is a sign of evolution in the development of a sense of belonging and social identity.

In Italy, archeologists found the oldest burial site in Europe. They found the bones of at least 22 human beings, many of them children, who died between 7,500 and 7,200 years ago. The bodies were buried in Scaloria Cave in the Tavoliere region (Southern Italy) (Shaw, 2015) and became the first documented remains of the first farmer community in the area. According to the reports, the bodies underwent the process of defleshing: "When people died, villagers stripped their bones bare, pulled them apart, and mingled them with animal remains in a nearby cave. The practice was meant to separate the dead from the living" (Shaw, 2015, para. 1).

The Italian Bronze Age

The Bronze Age was a stage of technological growth that developed out of the Neolithic and implied the use of bronze. This metal is obtained by alloying tin and copper at about 1742 °F. Then, artisans would mold the new metal and use it to manufacture weapons and tools instead of stone. It is associated with early European civilizations that lived in the 4th and 3rd millennia B.C.E. (Knowles, n.d.).

In Italy, the Bronze Age is dated between 2,300 and 950 B.C.E., and it concentrated in the wetland locations along the Alpine margin. It is believed that former communities inhabited the area, but there is no evidence. The oldest artifacts found in the area are axes, which were stored in a separate place from the settlement. These people also used amber and faience (glazed ceramics) to manufacture prestige artifacts, which revealed different social statuses.

Later, settlements in the Po Valley region increased. These banked and ditched settlements are called *Terramare*. The demographic density increased throughout the period, and the complex drainage works and the pile-built dwellings are signs of a highly organized society mainly dedicated to metal production (*The Italian Bronze Age*, n.d.).

In the central plains and the upper lands of the Apennines, the period is usually referred to as the Apennine Bronze Age (*The Italian Bronze Age*, n.d.). The remains show pastoralist communities. They also had levels of social status revealed by the burial rituals. According to the archeological findings, the warriors were at the top of the social pyramid. The evolution of the use of bronze is linked to trade with the cultures in the Aegean Sea – early Greeks.

Traders from the Aegean reached the southern coasts of Sicily and Sardinia. However, they also reached the north-central region of the Terramare by sea. There are Aegean pottery remains in northern Italy, and they reveal a vibrant trade relationship in the 13th and 12th centuries B.C.E.

The Nuragic Civilization: An Example of Indigenous Tribes

There were many prehistoric Italian cultures, each with its own distinctive styles of pottery, architecture, jewelry, weapons, and other artifacts. A survey of every group would be massive, but a short description of one culture might give the reader an impression of the richness of many ancient societies that are now lost to time.

Between the early Bronze Age and the 2nd century B.C.E., Nuragic civilization flourished on the islands of Corsica and Sardinia. These "prehistoric" people evolved before and during the Romans' hegemony in Italy.

This civilization owes its name to the towers they built, known as Nuraghe. They are examples of megalithic remains (monuments of stone with different meanings depending on the period and culture). Some theories suggest that these towers were used as fortresses, prisons, temples, or tombs (Ancos, 2018).

During the Bronze Age, Nuragic art depicted animals from Africa and weapons from the Aegean, which suggests contact with people from other lands. They were in touch with the Mycenaean Greeks, the

Egyptians of the New Kingdom, and later with the Phoenician and Greek colonial settlements around the Mediterranean (*Nuragic Monuments of Sardinia*, n.d.).

The Dawn of the Iron Age

The passage from one age into another didn't happen in a short period of time and in all regions simultaneously. Around the 13th century B.C.E., while many civilizations were still developing the use of bronze in Scandinavia and other areas of Europe, some discovered how to refine a new metal that was found in nature - iron. It was easier to find than copper but required kilns capable of much higher heat than those used for making bronze.

Once human beings mastered the metal, a true technological revolution started with significant consequences. The process of manufacturing weapons and tools became faster and cheaper; therefore, the number of products quickly increased. New and more sophisticated tools enabled an improvement in the production of everything and better infrastructure for towns.

Increased production capacity led to a rapid demographic increase, and that implied a higher pressure on the environment. More crops were needed to feed an increasing population; therefore, more trees were cut down to widen the farmland and to provide more wood to fuel the furnaces used to melt and shape iron. Wood was also used to manufacture weapons and tools, and the circle continued.

In the long term, the Bronze and Iron Ages witnessed an unprecedented demographic expansion and a large-scale technological revolution. Societies changed, and the emergent states began to fight each other to conquer lands and obtain resources that became progressively scarce.

The shift from bronze to iron introduced many changes in warfare. Its evolution coincides with the collapse of several important civilizations in the Bronze Age: the Egyptian, Mycenaean Greek, and Hittite cultures were in crisis caused by the so-called Sea People. This meant a reshaping of the Mediterranean world's balance of power.

Moreover, the discovery of iron changed the trading networks. The coastal settlements of Italy traded for bronze and iron with the Middle East, India, and the lands in between. Then, over the centuries, other goods were incorporated into a far-reaching network of trade routes (Sherry & Zamechek, n.d.).

The Iron Age in Italy

Between the 12th and 8th centuries B.C.E., different West Indo-European tribes entered and settled the Italian peninsula from the Po valley through the plains at the feet of the Apennines to the southern coasts. They interacted with the native tribes of Italy, including the Etruscans, whom we will discuss in depth in the following section.

The Indo-European tribes originated from the Balkan Peninsula and likely migrated there from the Pontic steppe, located on the northern coast of the Black Sea. They may have entered Italy from the northeast (Kessler & Dawson, 2019).

Many Indo-European groups arrived in Italy in the late Bronze and early Iron ages. The three most important for our purposes here are the Iapyges, Italics, and Greeks. The first group settled primarily in the southeast, in modern Apulia – the heel of Italy's boot. The Italics arrived about two centuries later and settled in the central plains at the foot of the Apennines (Kessler & Dawson, 2019).

Starting in the 8th century B.C.E., Greeks began to colonize the western Mediterranean. Their presence in the southern half of Italy was so widespread that the later Romans called southern Italy *Magna Graecia* – "Greater Greece." All three groups intermingled with the native population. Therefore, the tribes that lived in Italy during the early Iron Age were a mixture of immigrants and natives.

Finally, in the late Iron Age, another tribe coming from central Europe entered the peninsula through the Alps and pressured the populations living in the Po valley. They represent the Golasecca culture, and some of their descendants were known to the Romans as Ligurians. They remained present in the northwest of the peninsula and controlled the northern plains for several centuries (Kessler, n.d.).

The Iron Age includes all of ancient Roman history. For the duration of the Roman Monarchy and most of the Republic, the peninsula was a patchwork of many different cultures that exchanged ideas, goods, and resources – all mutually shaping one another. And they just as often went to war, eventually losing to, and being absorbed by, Rome. As one scholar has put it, "Politically, many of these people were fiercely inclined towards independence. At the same time, however, the diffusion of Hellenistic (Greek) ideas, fashions, and styles created a range of 'hybrid' cultures that were only unified by Rome" (Kamash et al., 2013, p. 336).

The Etruscans

One of the most important civilizations that lived on the Italian Peninsula during the early Iron Age was the Etruscans. Their origin was different from the other tribes described before, and there is no certainty about where they came from. They had unique practices, although they interacted with and received influence from the Greek colonists. For scholars, the origins and early history of the Etruscans remain a mystery.

This ancient civilization thrived in central Italy between the 11th and 9th centuries. After a long, slow decline in influence, they were eventually supplanted by the Romans in the 3rd century B.C.E. Genetic samples gathered by researchers indicate that the civilization flourished mostly in Etruria, modern Tuscany, and the island of Corsica.

Herodotus, the ancient Greek historian, argued that these people, who called themselves Rasenna, invaded Etruria from Anatolia before 800 B.C.E. and displaced the native population of the region. Other historians, instead, believed that they were native to the peninsula and that they were even the Sea People who caused the collapse of other ancient empires, including the Mycenaean Greeks and the Hittites (Comunale, 2022).

One of the greatest mysteries surrounding the Etruscans is related to their language. In the historical period, they were surrounded by Indo-European languages: the Greeks in the south, the Celtic Gauls in the north, and the Italic Umbrians, Samnites, Sabines, and Latins to the southeast (Comunale, 2022). Nonetheless, the Etruscan language didn't share the same Indo-European roots, and (if the prevalent modern theories are correct) it may have formed as a distinct member of the "Tyrsenian" language group by the 13th century B.C.E. Unfortunately, the Tyrsenian languages are all poorly attested, and the earliest Etruscan inscription dates from about 700 B.C.E.

One major theory hypothesizes that, during the late Bronze Age, they arrived from across the sea and established themselves in Tuscany, where they founded important cities such as Pisa, Bologna, and Capua. But the large number of Etruscan inscriptions isn't helpful. We cannot translate them with much certainty, and the language had largely fallen out of use by the 2nd century B.C.E., when Rome had absorbed the Etruscan people.

However, they had a large and long-lasting influence on other emerging civilizations in Italy: "It was from the Etruscans that the Romans inherited many of their own cultural and artistic traditions, from the spectacle of gladiatorial combat to hydraulic engineering, temple design, and religious ritual, among many other things" (Taylor & Brenan, n.d., para. 10).

Essential Highlights

Civilization on the Italian Peninsula started several centuries before the Romans emerged. Early Indo-European peoples reached these lands during the Bronze Age from the Aegean and Balkans by land and sea. They developed agriculture and animal husbandry, built the first large settlements, and formed the first complex societies.

Many of the original tribes would merge to form a new civilization: the Romans, who began as Latins, dominated their Italic neighbors, and eventually controlled all of Italy. The Etruscans, on the other hand, remained a distinct linguistic group that was later subdued by Rome.

Throughout this chapter, we outlined how different tribes interacted with each other through trade and cultural exchange. Technological evolution impacted demographics, influencing migration waves and human settlement patterns. It also strained natural resources. The shift in materials and strategies used for survival paved the way for Western civilization.

However, all the aspects covered in this chapter are what archeologists and scholars have taught us about prehistoric Italy. There is another history about the time when Rome still didn't exist—the history created and held by tradition. Roman mythology.

While prehistoric tribes intermingled and paved their paths, a legend was born. Two twins, abandoned to die in the wild, were raised by a she-wolf, the totem animal of Mars, god of war. Later, they laid the foundations of the city that would conquer and rule this landscape. In the next chapter, we will discuss the earliest legends of Rome - how Romulus and Remus founded Rome and established the monarchy.

Chapter 2: The Founding of Rome

Rome was not built in a day. –Marcus Tullius
Cicero

Rome, the city, and its civilization weren't the
products of an overnight process. It was the outcome
of a complex of tradition, myths, and cultural
integration among people with different
backgrounds.

Nations' identities are a combination of historical
facts, reliable evidence, and a sense of belonging that
is usually based on a mythical origin. The legend of
Romulus and Remus explains the origins of not only
Rome but all the Latin tribes (of which the Romans
were a part). Early Roman identity was a mix of
native and imported cultures, formed over centuries
of migration waves, and consisting (mainly) of
Etruscan, Italic, and Aegean influences.

The Founding Myth

The Romans traced their ancestry back to Aeneas, one of the many heroes of Homer's *Iliad*, one of
the two great epics of Greece's most important poet
(~8th century B.C.E.). Aeneas fought for Troy (modern Hissarlik, Turkey) against invading Greeks. After
a ten-year siege, the Greeks stormed, pillaged, and
torched the city.

The image of Aeneas carrying his elderly father and the statues of their family gods out of the inferno has inspired artists for millennia, and greatly impressed the Romans. If factual, the Trojan War likely occurred between 1,200 and 1,150 B.C.E. – the archaeology of the site preserves scorch marks and possible evidence of attack.

Many centuries later, the Roman historians Livy (Titus Livius, 59 B.C.E. – 17 C.E.) and Dionysius of Halicarnassus (ca. 60 – 7 B.C.E.) tied Aeneas to Rome's founding with slight variations. Dionysius offers more detail. However, the elegance and drama of Livy's prose helped define Golden Age Latin literature. The following excerpts from Livy trace Aeneas' adventures in Italy and the foundation of Rome by his descendants, Romulus and Remus. They are edited for brevity.

Aeneas Arrives in Italy

"The consensus is that most Trojans met a savage end after their city was captured. However, the Greeks showed mercy to Aeneas. Ultimately, the Fates led him to greater deeds. First, he came to Macedonia (north of Greece), then to Sicily, looking for a home. Finally, he reached Laurentum with his fleet (an early Latin coastal town).

With nothing left after their wandering but their weapons and ships, Aeneas' men plundered the fields. But King Latinus and the Aborigines who occupied the land rushed from their city and crops and armed themselves to fend off the violent invaders. The opposing armies formed up for battle; however, before sounding the charge, Latinus advanced with his nobles and called the leader of the invaders to a meeting.

He asked who they were, from where or for what reason they had left home, and what they sought in the land of Laurentum. He learned that they were Trojans, that Aeneas, son of Anchises and Venus (the Greek Aphrodite), was their leader, and that they had fled their devastated homeland and now wanted to found a city. Amazed by Aeneas and his divine parent, and how he seemed equally disposed to war or peace, Latinus offered his right hand in friendship.

Aeneas became a guest in Latinus' house, and the king forged a family alliance by giving Aeneas his daughter Lavinia in marriage. The Trojans founded a town, and Aeneas named it Lavinium in honor of his wife. Soon, a child was born whom they named Ascanius.

Turnus, king of the Rutulians, waged war upon both Aeneas and Latinus, for Lavinia had been promised to him before Aeneas' arrival. The Rutulians were defeated, but the Aborigines and Trojans lost Latinus, their king.

The demoralized Rutulians fled with Turnus to the rich and powerful Etruscans and their king, Mezentius who then ruled the wealthy port city of Caere (modern Cerveteri, 35 miles north-northwest of Rome). The Etruscan leader had not been pleased by the birth of Aeneas' new city, and he felt Trojans were growing too quickly and endangering their neighbors. Therefore, he willingly forged an alliance with the Rutulians.

To overcome the Aborigines' fear of such a war, and to give them the same name, Aeneas called upon Trojans and Aborigines both as Latins. Thereafter, the Aborigines matched the Trojans in fondness of and faith in Aeneas.

The Trojan hero led forth his army even though the reputation of Etruria's power filled the length and breadth of Italy from the Alps to the Sicilian Strait. The outcome favored the Latins, but it was the last of Aeneas' mortal deeds. He lies by the river Numicus.

Ascanius left Lavinium to his mother when its population grew too large – it was already a flourishing and wealthy city – and he founded a new settlement near Mount Albanus called Alba Longa. Peace prevailed between the Latins and Etruscans, with the river Albula, which we now call the Tiber, forming the border." (Livy, 1.1-2 abridged)

Romulus, Remus, and the Founding of Rome

"[Eleven generations passed before violence grew] more powerful than family duty or respect for seniority (cf. Whelan, 2020; García, 2018). Amulius ruled Alba Longa after he expelled his elder brother, Numitor, from the city. He heaped crime upon crime, first murdering his nephew, then depriving his niece Rhea Silvia of the hope of motherhood (*Romulus and Remus: The Story of the Founding of Rome*, 2016).

He enforced her chastity by making her a Vestal Virgin, a pretext rather than an honor.

The Vestal was ravished by force, and after she gave birth to twins, she claimed Mars was the father. Amulius ordered the priestess to be chained up in prison and the children thrown into the river. But, when the slow-moving water stranded the floating basket that held the boys on a dry patch, a thirsty she-wolf from the surrounding mountains turned to their plaintive cries. She nursed them so tenderly that the master of the royal flock, Faustulus, found her caressing the infants with her tongue.

He brought them to the house he shared with his wife, Larentia. As soon as they were able, they wandered the woods to hunt, but they neglected neither their homestead nor its flocks. In addition to wild animals, they attacked bandits carrying loot and shared it with neighboring shepherds – the youthful band of Romulus and Remus grew day by day.

Angry because of their lost loot, some bandits ambushed the brothers. Romulus fought them off by force, but they captured Remus and handed him over to King Amulius. The main crime, they claimed, was that the brothers attacked Numitor's fields, pillaging them with a band of young men as if they were an enemy army. Therefore, Remus was sent to Numitor for punishment.

Now, Faustulus knew that a pair of infants had been exposed by order of the king. Moreover, the time he himself rescued the twins corresponded exactly. Therefore, he fearfully told Romulus the truth of the matter. Numitor, too, was reminded of his grandsons when he held Remus in custody and heard he had a twin brother. He drew the same conclusion as Faustulus, and thus King Amulius' misdeeds now surrounded him on both sides.

Romulus was not in favor of open war, so he did not assemble his entire band. Instead, he chose a select few to make their way covertly to the palace at an appointed time and attack the king. Remus supported him with another force he had gathered from the house of Numitor, and thus Romulus slew his great uncle, Amulius.

Numitor called a council and laid out his brother's crimes against him, the lineage of his grandsons, and how they were born, raised, and revealed. When the youths pushed through the council with their band and saluted Numitor as king, the shout of agreement from the crowd confirmed his title and power.

Thereafter, Romulus and Remus were seized by the desire to found a city near where they were exposed and raised. However, since they were twins and respect for seniority was unable to make a distinction between them, they agreed that the gods should dictate through bird signs who would name the new city and rule it. Romulus took the Palatine hill as his place to perform the auguries (a ritual to interpret bird signs), Remus the Aventine.

A sign first came to Remus – six vultures. Yet, as soon as this was reported, twice as many revealed themselves to Romulus. Each twin's followers proclaimed him king - Remus claimed kingship based on when his sign appeared, Romulus on the number of birds. They fought first with words before turning to violence, and Remus fell, struck down in the melee.

A more common report is that Remus vaulted over the city's new wall in mockery of his brother. The enraged Romulus killed him as he shouted, 'Thus shall die anyone who should leap over my walls!' Romulus alone took power, and the new city took the name of its founder." (Livy, 1.3-7 abridged)

Later Roman tradition dated the founding to 753 B.C.E. (Encyclopaedia Britannica, 2023).

Proximity to Contemporary Greek Culture

It is unknown when this story was told for the first time. However, it reveals the deep influence of the ancient Greeks on Roman culture. The god Mars is the Roman version of the Greek god of war, Ares, and their mother, Rhea, shares the name of a Greek Titan, the mother of Zeus and the other gods.

It isn't coincidental that a she-wolf was the animal that saved Rome's founder. The she-wolf represented one of Mars' (Ares') sacred animals. Somehow, it symbolized that Rome—and therefore, Romans—were Mars' people. Their entire history bears this out.

The myth explains the origins of the political community and provides it with legitimacy. The destiny and the actions of the twins, and therefore their people, were ordained by the gods. It played an important role in the constitution of political power and, later, in the establishment of the Republic and Empire.

In addition to Livy, this legend and the origins of Rome were linked to Hellenistic (Greek) culture by the Roman poet Virgil. Like Homer, Virgil wrote poetry that helped define the identity of his society. Among other poems, he wrote the *Aeneid*, an epic that tells Aeneas' story, consciously tying it to the social and political structures of the early Roman Empire.

The Aeneid was written by order of Rome's first emperor, Augustus, at an inflection point in Roman history when the Empire was being built. This fact illustrates two important aspects of Rome's founding mythology. First, the story that blended Italic, Etruscan, and Greek elements was an integral part of Roman identity by the 1st century B.C.E., if not long before – it was the Romans' national story.

Second, the tradition was so fundamental that, at least in Augustus' mind, manipulating it had the power to permanently reshape Roman society. The third part of this book analyzes how history, popular culture, and oral tradition blend to shape a nation's identity, often influenced by political and social motivations (Vandiver, n.d.).

The Roman Kingdom

The Historical Foundation of Rome

While we can't settle on a precise foundation date for the city, most scholars accept the Roman calculation of 753 B.C.E. as an acceptable ballpark figure, if too precise. Nevertheless, archeological findings reveal that the first political regime at Rome was a monarchy. Most civilizations in the early first millennium B.C.E. developed around a principal city and had concentrated power – a city-state. Most city-states initially formed under the centralized power of a king.

In Italy, several excavations have exposed the ruins of the Regia, the king's house. In addition, archeologists have found a cup with the word *rex* (king in Latin) inscribed on it, and it was dated to the 7th century. There was also an inscription on the *Lapis Niger* (the Black Rock), a shrine in the Roman Forum, with the word *recei* (an archaic form of *rex*). The inscription is difficult to interpret, but many scholars believe it was probably a law (*Ancient Roman Monarchy*, n.d.).

According to the tradition, after founding Rome, Romulus invited merchants and men from all walks of life to join his new community. He recognized them all as citizens with equal rights, and all of them agreed to appoint him as their king. That is how the monarchy was established in Rome.

Unlike many other ancient civilizations, Roman kings didn't necessarily belong to a hereditary nobility, nor did they rely on a military caste that supported them. People elected them, and they served as kings for the rest of their lives. Twelve bodyguards called lictors accompanied the king. They each bore a bundle of wooden rods surrounding an axe – the *fasces*. These were stark visual symbols of the king's *imperium*, his power to command obedience. The rods could compel; the axe could execute. The later Roman magistrates vested with *imperium*, were similarly accompanied, though their power of command was limited to a specific task or geographical region – a *provincia*, or province. The term *Imperium Romanum* came to denote the regions subject to the commands of a Roman magistrate. Its direct English equivalent – Roman Empire.

Roman kings sat in a curule (usually foldable) chair and wore the purple *toga picta* (colored toga) and red shoes. Instead of a metal crown, they wore a white diadem made of wool or linen around their heads (*The Roman Kingdom*, n.d.). These physical objects symbolized their royal authority and sovereignty. Their origin seems to have been Etruscan.

Social Hierarchical Organization

The growing city was organized as a monarchy. Its founder, Romulus, gave citizenship to all the people who joined him, and, in turn, they elected him as the first monarch. It set the basis for the monarchy going forward: "The kingdom was established by unanimous acclaim with him at the helm when Romulus called the citizenry to a council to determine their government" (*The Roman Kingdom*, n.d., para. 5).

Roman society organized itself as a fixed hierarchy that reflected its values and ensured its political unity. Hierarchies rank people according to their power, status, or privileges. This inequality was accepted by Roman society.

The nuclear unit of ancient Roman society was the family, and it influenced all the other institutions of the political system. It was the cornerstone of the whole social pyramid and was also hierarchically organized (Schultz, 2019).

Even though the word "family" comes from the Latin word *familia* they carry slightly different meanings. The Roman *familia* was a complete social and political unit led by the *paterfamilias* ("the father of the family," a head of the household); thus, it was patriarchal. He formally owned the family's property and was the source of family law.

There were three types of familial bonds (Schultz, 2019):

- the agnates (*agnati*): Relatives by blood or adoption through the father's line, the *paternum gens*.

- the cognates (*cognati*): All relatives, including the *maternum gens*, that is through the mother's line.
- and *affines/adfines*: Those related by marriage, like brothers-in-law.

Each category had a particular political role within the family and society. The agnates could inherit property and, in this capacity, enjoyed the full benefits of Roman citizenship. They were the only ones who could inherit the *paterfamilias'* power, called *patria potestas*. It allowed them to celebrate contracts, lend, mortgage, and interact with other families through their respective *patresfamilias*.

A *familia* was self-sufficient, and each *paterfamilias* had full authority over its members, including the power of life and death. Yet, tradition imposed the moral imperative to provide for and protect the welfare of the *familia* upon the *paterfamilias*. An unduly tyrannical (by Roman standards) head of the household would face social and religious blowback for failing to look after his responsibilities. Therefore, Roman society was a complex network of extended families, each ruled by a head. This patriarchal organization defined relationships between families as well.

Often, the heads of weaker, poorer, or less illustrious households would ally themselves with the heads of more powerful families. The more powerful *paterfamilias* would become a *patronus* (patron – note the shared root *pat-* denoting the superior role) of the weaker, who would be called a *cliens* (client) of his superior. For most of Roman history, *clientes* were expected to support their *patroni* politically, electorally, or even physically, while the patrons would protect their clients from legal action or otherwise promote their welfare. The relationship was fundamental, and relied on *fides*, or faithfulness. This critical value was religiously grounded, and failing to maintain *fides* was generally considered a serious taboo.

This patriarchal structure permeated the Roman worldview. As a result, and as later chapters will show, it extended to Roman foreign policy. To the Roman mind, Rome was always the *patronus*. As a rule, it would form treaties with individual city-states or tribes as a powerful head of household would pledge to protect a weaker client. Of course, the arrangement always favored Rome, but the client states often enjoyed more safety, stability, and prosperity as tributaries. Besides, the *fides* of the Romans often made them reliable friends. However, the idea is abstract, and many tribes and city-states found themselves the subjects of Roman anger when they may have followed a treaty to the letter, but did not satisfy the Roman definition of *fides*.

At the bottom of the social scale, there were slaves and freedmen. Slavery was a common practice in antiquity. Slaves were former war prisoners or people with unpaid debts. At the early stage of the Roman civilization, slaves weren't massively exploited. However, they were considered part of the *paterfamilias'* property (Schultz, 2019).

Slaves could achieve manumission and become freedmen or freedwomen. They became free, able to vote, and otherwise participate in Roman society. However, they could not hold political office beyond low-level local magistracies. Moreover, they would immediately become a client of their former owner. (Schultz, 2019).

Fundamental Roman Values

For Romans, social order was closely linked to their moral background, which was rooted in traditions. This first stage of the life of Rome was mainly based on customary law. They followed the rules of traditions: It was good because it had been used before. They used the term *mos maiorum*, or "the customs of the ancestors" (Jasiński, 2020).

As explained before, *fides* was an essential value for ancient Romans. A citizen's word was enough to create a formal obligation or institute a contract. However, *fides* also applied to informal promises that should be held and fulfilled.

Another core value was bravery. It was considered a virtue, a concept that originally came from the word *vir* (husband, man, or hero), thus it was associated with masculinity. It meant having the ability to distinguish good from bad and fight against evil. In war, it was considered a virtue to fight bravely against Rome's enemies.

Women weren't excluded from this value, but for them, being brave implied remaining attached to Roman traditions and being an exemplary wife and mother. That was her role within a patriarchy (Jasiński, 2020). The mother of the family was the *materfamilias,* and along with their husband and other free adult members of the household, they were the family council (*concilium*) (Schultz, 2019).

Piety, *pietas,* was another foundational value. It encompassed the worship of Roman deities, strict attachment to their traditions, and dedication to family, which had to instruct future generations in those traditions. Consider, again, how powerfully the image of Aeneas carrying his father and the statues of their family gods out of burning Troy struck the Romans.

Seriousness, or *gravitas,* was self-control as a means of respect for social conventions and morality. Romans repressed their emotions in public, for instance, expressions of anger or affection. Those were preserved in the private realm.

Then, they valued respect and worthiness: *dignitas.* Women had to bear their husbands' children and carry with dignity all their responsibilities as mothers and wives. Men, on their end, held the position they had within a hierarchical society: they had to show that position and honor it, respecting others while also demanding respect from their subordinates. Often, the number and power of a man's clients was a measure of his *dignitas.*

Last but not least, authority: *auctoritas* was of utmost importance in a hierarchical society. It came along with *dignitas* in the case of men, who had the power to give orders and be obeyed. It was associated with personal relationships and honor rather than formal laws.

Rome's Unique Inclusivity

Early Roman society was quite small and interacted freely with the neighboring tribes. As explained earlier, different communities interacted with each other and not only exchanged and traded goods but also shared knowledge. They shaped each other's culture and cooperated in development.

Many early Romans were former people from other tribes who gathered to create a new political community. According to the foundational myth, Rome was founded by Romulus, a refugee, and the people who accompanied him after killing the king. Therefore, they had a unique perception of the foreigner. This conception made Romans more welcoming to foreigners and allowed many newcomers to achieve the status of a Roman citizen, which wasn't common in many other ancient civilizations (Beard, 2018).

Since the earliest Romans were a handful of families who settled among the hills near the Tiber, they needed others to make the community grow. Therefore, they developed an inclusive foreign affairs management system. They interacted with other cultures and later conquered many of them, but they didn't destroy their institutions or forbid their traditions. The Romans were devoted to traditions. Instead, they blended. When Rome became more powerful, Latin culture eventually became predominant throughout Italy, but this policy of inclusivity was one of the pillars of Rome's power and stability.

Inclusivity was crucial for the early Roman kingdom's development. It enabled foreigners to become citizens, which is important not only to support demographic expansion but also for economic and military reasons. The Romans were open enough to accept the idea of a foreigner as ruler – they may even have had a Greek king. According to legend, in the 6th century, Lucius Tarquinius Priscus became the 5th king of Rome. His original name was Tarquin, and his father was a Greek who had migrated to Tarquinii, an Etruscan city. The family moved to Rome, and Tarquin, who changed his name to Lucius Tarquinius (a Latin name), became the guardian of the sons of King Ancus Marcius. Later, Tarquin became king of Rome although he was a Greco-Etruscan immigrant. The story may belong in part to mythology, but there is some archeological evidence supporting the existence of the Tarquins during the period (Encyclopaedia Britannica, 1998).

Early Sabine Integration

Despite this inclusive nature of the Romans, we should not downplay their tendency to assert their patriarchal worldview by force. A controversial episode at the earliest stage of Roman history serves as a colorful illustration. It involved a neighboring tribe, the Sabines. The legendary Rape of the Sabine Women, as the event is called, took place around 750 B.C.E., shortly after the city was founded.

The Sabines lived on the Italian peninsula, on the east bank of the Tiber River, along the Apennine ridge. There is limited evidence of their original language, which was probably Oscan, but only some of their dialect survived and many of the words were adopted by Latin speakers (Tikkanen, 2022). Scholars believe the Sabines belonged to the same ethnic group as the Samnites and Sabellians. They were Italic, and distantly related to the Latins since they all shared Indo-European roots (*The Sabines: A Glimpse into an Ancient Italic Tribe*, 2023).

The Greek biographer Plutarch told the story of a strategy deployed by Romulus to provide the men of his kingdom with wives since there were no women in their community. Without women, the community was doomed.

Plutarch wrote that Romulus invited the Sabines to a banquet in Rome during a festival of the god Neptune Equester. During the feast, the Romans dashed in and kidnapped the women. Then, the

Sabine women were kept as captives and forced to take Romans as husbands (David, 2013).

Livy also wrote about the abduction of the Sabines. According to him, Romulus was concerned about the decline in the birth rate within the young community and attempted to make arrangements with neighboring tribes to make women marry Roman men. Since their neighbors refused to accept the deal, they were compelled to plan the abduction of the Sabine women (Sal, 2020).

Both authors Plutarch and Livy, agreed in pointing out that after the abduction of the Sabine women, a war was started between both communities, but the women interceded to stop the attacks.

The Sabine influence can be found in two of the first four kings of Rome, Numa Pompilius and Ancus Marcius, and also in one of the three names of the original tribes of Rome: the *Tities*. The other two tribes, the *Ramnes* and *Luceres*, supposedly represented the early city's other two predominant ethnic groups, the Latins and Etruscans, respectively.

Furthermore, many Sabine family names appear in prominent positions throughout Roman history. Many Roman families had traditional connections going back centuries, presumably to a theoretical common ancestor. A group of families connected in this way was called a *gens*, or clan. Several influential Roman *gentes* had a Sabine origin: *gens Curtia, gens Pompilia, gens Marcia,* and *gens Claudia* (*The Sabines: A Glimpse into an Ancient Italic Tribe,*

2023). The first dynasty of Roman emperors bears the name Julio-Claudian because the emperor Augustus' successor, his adopted son Tiberius, belonged to the *gens Claudia*.

The Sabine cities didn't disappear after many Sabines inhabited Rome, and the tense relationship continued through the 5th and the 3rd centuries B.C.E. (*The Sabines: A Glimpse into an Ancient Italic Tribe*, 2023). There were many battles between both societies, but the interaction between them became regular over time, and the Sabines were eventually fully absorbed by the Romans by 290 B.C.E. (Tikkanen, 2022). At that point, they all became full Roman citizens.

Essential Highlights

Legend and historical evidence blend to explain the origins of the Eternal City. The strength of both components reveals the power of tradition and heritage within ancient Roman society. The attachment to their mythical origin and the cultural legacy that made them what they became is rooted in the backbone of their society.

The new city became a monarchy, but one based on strong values that ensured unity. As a kingdom, it relied on the solid bonds of the most important institution: family. Then, it evolved into a powerful civilization capable of conquering and subjugating neighboring tribes, not to destroy them but to incorporate them into their growing society.

Romulus was the first king, the founder, and the one accountable for setting the foundations of the monarchy, but... who were the subsequent rulers that helmed the burgeoning empire? In the next chapter, we'll delve deep into the reigns and realms of the 7 Kings of Rome.

Chapter 3: The 7 Kings of Rome

History is filled with the sound of silken slippers going downstairs and wooden shoes coming up. –Voltaire

Unraveling Myth from History

The study of ancient history poses certain challenges to historians. Ancient civilizations at their early stages, like the moment of the foundation of Rome, didn't have a systematized procedure to record facts and events. The concepts of history and science hadn't been developed yet. Therefore, historians rely upon archeological findings and attempt to rebuild that part of history by interpreting those findings (*Online Ancient History Undergraduate Tutors Spires*, n.d.).

On some occasions, what is known about the distant past with no written records is based on what later writers from those societies told about their past. That is the case of Homer and his *Iliad* and *Odyssey* in ancient Greece, or the works of Virgil and Plutarch in ancient Rome. It is almost impossible to distinguish between what happened and what was created by popular imagination.

For those societies, there was a blurry line between historical facts and popular beliefs transmitted through oral traditions. Reality blended with myths and mystical explanations, and it was part of their daily lives. Therefore, it can be accepted that ancient history is a combination of what history as a modern discipline can prove and what is taken from ancient people's own perceptions of their past (*Online Ancient History Undergraduate Tutors Spires*, n.d.). Moreover, their perception can be shaped by cultural or political bias. Even so, it is still a valuable source of information about the past because it gives us insight into their cultural, intellectual, and literary history.

The legend of Romulus and Remus hasn't been proven with empirical evidence. It "probably originated in the 4th century B.C.E and was set down in coherent form at the end of the 3rd century B.C.E. It contains a mixture of Greek and Roman elements"

(Encyclopaedia Britannica, 2023, para. 5). Although there is no empirical evidence of Romulus and Remus' existence or their relationship with a she-wolf, it is still part of Rome's history. Indeed, it would be difficult to argue that the idea of Romulus had less far-reaching consequences for Roman society than, say, a historical figure like Pompey the Great – as important as he was.

The two centuries following Rome's foundation present these complexities. There is little evidence about the monarchy and the first rulers. However, we tend to include Romulus as the first of the seven ancient kings. There is enough evidence to assert the final three were likely historical, and many historians also believe the first three after Romulus existed (*Ancient Roman Monarchy*, n.d.). Most of them appear in literature from different periods of Rome's history, and archeological remains sometimes seem to support their existence (Marta, 2021).

Having said this, let's proceed into what historians have learned about the first rulers of the civilization that grew to dominate the known world. It is inevitably the result of blending historical facts discovered by historians and archeologists with myths and legends from the Romans' self-reflections on their own past (Marta, 2021).

The First Kings of Rome

Most historians agree to mention seven kings: "Romulus (753–716 B.C.E.), Numa Pompilius (715–

673 B.C.E.), Tullus Hostilius (673–641 B.C.E.), Ancus Marcius (641–616 B.C.E.), Tarquinius Priscus (616–579 B.C.E.), Servius Tullius (578–535 B.C.E.) and Tarquinius Superbus (535–509 B.C.E.)" (The Roman Kingdom, n.d., para. 3). The number seven had a special symbolism for ancient Romans since it is also present in the seven hills where Rome was founded (Gill, 2019).

Other historians include an eighth king, Titus Tatius. He was the Sabine ruler when the Romans kidnapped the Sabine women. According to some scholars, the conflict between both communities was resolved with a dual monarchy: Romulus and Titus Tatius. This regime lasted a few years until Titus Tatius was killed by a mob, but it further supports the early integration of the Sabines with the Romans (Encyclopaedia Britannica, 1998). Even though Titus Tatius is usually left off the list of Roman monarchs, he is credited by tradition for establishing altars to many Sabine deities that were later included in Roman religion.

Romulus

His arrival to power was framed by bloodshed and hate, and he emerged as a single leader after killing his brother Remus. As a ruler, he "kept his guards close, and his enemies closer—after all, founding a culture on the blood of your twin brother does not give the people you are ruling any sort of comfort" (Winters, 2019, para. 3).

His first acts of government were focused on ensuring the growth and stability of the city's population. He came back to his birthplace and gathered men to join him. Later, he arranged the episode with the Sabines that secured wives for the male population – albeit by force. He may have shared power for a while with the Sabine king, Titus Tatius, until he was assassinated, and Romulus became the sole ruler again.

Besides establishing the fundamental political institutions of Rome, like the Senate (see below), he led the first expansion of the city through war and conquest. After Numitor's death, Romulus incorporated Alba Longa, the semi-legendary Latin city founded by his ancestor Ascanius, son of Aeneas. In addition, he formed alliances with neighboring settlements like Lavinium, the town founded by Aeneas himself (Garcia, 2018).

The end of Romulus' reign remains shrouded in mystery. Some people claimed to have witnessed how he was lifted to heaven and became a god. Another hypothesis poses he was killed by a senatorial conspiracy. It is known that "Romulus disappeared in 717 B.C.E., as reported by Plutarch, at the age of 53, but Dionysius of Halicarnassus reports that he died at the age of 55" (García, 2018, para. 9).

Numa Pompilius

After Romulus' death, there was an *interregnum* of a year. During that time "between the reigns," an *interrex* would hold power for 5 days. Their mandate was to oversee the election of a new king and, if they were unable to do so, another *interrex* would be appointed. The process repeated until the election of a new king by the Senate. The extraordinary office of *interrex* survived down to the end of the Republic, and kept the state functioning in times of turmoil. Eventually, the Senate chose Numa Pompilius. He was a Sabine man who at first was reluctant to accept the offer but eventually agreed to it after consulting with the goddess Egeria (Vučkovič, 2023).

He was a strict and wise ruler who introduced several political, religious, and social reforms. He formulated a calendar of 12 months based on the moon's cycle and established the Vestal Virgins, and cults of Mars, Jupiter, and the deified Romulus (Quirinus). Unlike his predecessor, he advocated for peace.

He is credited with writing the first laws of Rome based on justice and equity and creating the concept of private property. He founded religious colleges and built many temples (Gill, 2019). His kingdom was one of splendor and prosperity.

Whether Numa actually lived is a matter of debate. He is mentioned by Plutarch and Livy, and his figure is exalted as a great and virtuous king who contributed to the greatness of Rome. According to these historians' versions, he reigned for over 40 years and died at the age of 81 (Vučkovič, 2023).

Tullus Hostilius

Very little is known about Tullus Hostilius. His existence is also open to debate. Historians assume he was elected by the Senate after Numa's death and that by then, the population of Rome had doubled.

Tullus is remembered as a warrior king, like Romulus. He destroyed Alba Longa and several other neighboring cities like Fidenae and Veii. He also compelled more Sabines to integrate into Rome. He is credited with building the first Senate House, initially called the *Curia Hostilia*, where the Roman Forum stands at present (Winters, 2019).

Unlike his predecessor, he neglected proper worship of the Roman gods. Livy said that at the end of his reign, Tullus grew very ill and begged for help from the gods. Jupiter, instead, threw a bolt of lightning that burned the king and his house to ashes (*The Seven Kings*, n.d.).

Ancus Marcius

There is also little historical evidence of his existence or of his reign beyond what ancient Roman historians tell us. However, he was an influential figure in the Roman consciousness at least until the late Republic. There is a reference to his name, for instance, in a silver denarius found in archeological excavations, dated from 57 B.C.E.

Ancus Marcius was Numa Pompilius's grandson and is credited for publishing his grandfather's religious works. However, Ancus was a warrior king who promoted the kingdom's expansion by conquering the Latin cities nearby and forcing their population to move into Rome (Winters, 2019).

Reforms During the Monarchy

The first rulers shaped the formal institutions of the Monarchy and set the foundations of a growing city-state. Their mandates were characterized by their contributions to the institutional organization of the government and the buildings constructed under their rule.

Unlike contemporary monarchies, these kings didn't belong to or establish a dynasty. Each of them was elected by the people. Romulus was directly elected by the people of Rome; the others were elected by deliberative or legislative bodies like the Senate and Curiate Assembly (see below, Chapter 4) (*The Seven Kings*, nd.). The hereditary nature of the throne was only established after the 5th king.

Once elected, kings had near absolute power and had the authority to pass laws, control the army, and be the supreme judges (Johnson, n.d.). However, Romans soon developed representative institutions and established a source of popular participation. The Senate and the Curiate Assembly were created during the first decades of the monarchy and although they had limited powers, it was a counterbalance to the king's supreme power. Despite his near-complete control, the king needed the assembly's support to declare war. When necessary, the Senate proposed the new king and the Curiate Assembly voted - these institutions were the ultimate source of the king's power (Winters, 2019).

The Senate

This institution is almost as ancient as Rome, since Romulus created it from the first citizens after being appointed king. It is also the most permanent element throughout Roman history, although its power, influence, and function changed throughout the different periods, and its essence has survived until the present. The word senate derives from the Latin word *senex*, which means old man. Therefore, the Senate was the assembly of the more experienced members of the community, a tradition inherited from the ancient Indo-European tribes, which were ruled by aristocratic groups of the oldest and (presumably) wisest men (Vermeulen, 2020).

Romulus chose 100 men to act as his advisory council. Each was a *paterfamilias*, and members of their families were thereafter called patricians, the privileged class (Vermeulen, 2020). Observe again the *pat-* root, denoting fatherhood. Indeed, later senators were often addressed as *patres*, fathers on the Senate floor. They represented their ancient tribes and held their power until they died (Encyclopaedia Britannica, 2023).

The Senate's power was indefinite and mainly consisted of providing advice to the king, but they had the last word to select the new ruler. After Romulus' death, the power reverted to the community embodied in the Senate, and their primary responsibility became keeping the state stable during the *interregnum* (Vermeulen, 2020).

Later, king Lucius Tarquinius Priscus (see below) chose 100 more senators from non-patrician families, and the number of senators increased. By 509 B.C.E., the Senate was composed of 300 members, patricians, and men from lesser families. Lucius Tarquinius Superbus, the last of the seven kings, executed many of the senators and didn't replace them with new members (Winters, 2019). This ushered in the decline of the Monarchy. After the Monarchy was replaced by the Republic, the Senate changed in composition and political role within the Roman system.

The Three Etruscan Kings

The Etruscans were introduced in Chapter 1 as people with uncertain origins who reached the Italian Peninsula before Rome's foundation and established themselves in central-western Italy (present-day Tuscany) and the island of Corsica. Their culture flourished between 700 and 500 B.C.E. which coincides with Rome's monarchical period.

For about 150 years, the Etruscans were raided by Celtic tribes from the north and engaged in several wars with the Romans. Both cultures coexisted and interacted intensely as the Romans acquired many of the Etruscans' institutions and cultural features. In fact, many of the patrician families of early Rome were Etruscan: "Examples include the *gens Herminia*, the *gens Lartia*, the *gens Tarquitia*, the *gens Verginia,* and the *gens Volumnia*" (Howells, 2023, para. 3). This phenomenon further reinforces the open nature of early Roman society – Rome may have had a Latin core, but the Sabine and Etruscan elements were strong from the earliest period.

By the middle of the 7th century B.C.E., Rome still had a small population with a citizen militia army, mainly composed of shepherds and farmers. However, its tendency to absorb people from among its neighbors meant that it grew quickly. Nevertheless, some historians believe that the Etruscans eventually took control of the Roman population, moved by their interest in the resources in and around the Roman hills. Rome was attractive because it was near the Tiber, it was easy to defend, and there were salt works nearby. In the ancient world, salt was a tremendously valuable commodity. The Etruscans were warriors, much like the Romans, and they also raided other tribes to expand their territory or take plunder.

At the end of the 7th century, the Etruscans had consolidated their place in Roman society. According to ancient Roman sources, the last three of the seven kings were Etruscan and played a key role in shaping Roman culture. Whether this represents a hostile takeover of Rome or is merely more evidence of

Rome's tendency to be free with its citizenship is an ongoing debate.

Lucius Tarquinius Priscus

His Latin name was Lucius Tarquinus Priscus, though his Etruscan name was likely Lucomo; however, this may have been a title instead of a name. He is accepted as the 5th king of Rome and was in power between 616 and 578 B.C.E. As noted above in Chapter 2, Tarquin was a Greek man's son who lived in Etruria and moved to Rome on his wife's urging. He was appointed as a royal guard, and when the king died, he lobbied the Senate, securing election over the former king Ancus Marcius' sons.

During his reign, the kingdom expanded its lands, and he added 100 senators. He was the first king to establish circus games as public entertainment. He is credited for some early monumental buildings such as the Temple of Jupiter Capitolinus and the *Cloaca Maxima*, Rome's massive sewer system (Gill, 2019).

Servius Tullius

Tarquinius Priscus was eventually killed by the sons of Ancus Marcius, and he was followed in office by his son-in-law, Servius Tullius. The 6th king of Rome carried out successful military campaigns that provided him with the resources to build the first stone fortification of the city: walls that encompassed the 7 hills of the early city. Remains of the so-called "Servian Wall" have been uncovered, but their construction likely dates from the early 4th century B.C.E., two centuries after Tullius' reign.

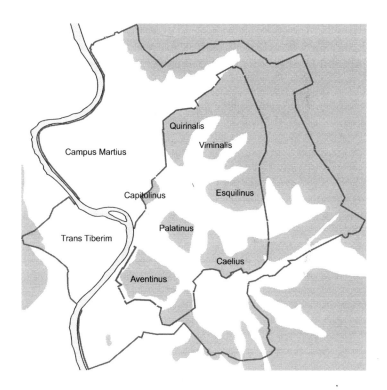

Later Romans attributed several important reforms to Servius Tullius. He instituted the first census, reformed the tribal system, and fixed the military obligations of 5 census-determined economic classes. (Gill, 2019). He set the basis for a new constitution with different rights for citizens regarding social classes: "Servius's reforms brought about a major change in Roman life—voting rights were now based on socioeconomic status, transferring much of the power into the hands of the Roman elite" (*The Seven Kings*, 2020, para. 19).

He reigned for 44 years and was murdered in a conspiracy. It was carried out by his daughter Tullia and her husband Lucius Tarquinius Superbus who wanted to seize power for himself (*The Seven Kings*, 2020).

Lucius Tarquinius Superbus

Tarquinius seized power after killing his father-in-law. He also made efforts to extend the kingdom's lands and continued to fight against neighboring tribes. Even though he carried out a few important public works, his reign is remembered for corruption and violence. He turned his back on the Senate and the Roman traditions, concentrating all the power in his hands.

In 509 B.C.E., a revolution led by Lucius Junius Brutus compelled Tarquinius and his family to flee from Rome. The trigger was the rape of Lucretia, by Tarquinius' son. She was the wife of Tarquinius' own nephew, Lucius Tarquinius Collatinus. After the king's expulsion, Brutus and Collatinus became the first consuls, the chief executives of the Republic (*The Seven Kings*, 2020).

Tarquinius' terrible reign left Rome with a negative view of monarchy, and, for many generations, the Romans would avoid any semblance of one-man rule. Indeed, accusing a Roman politician of aiming at *regnum* was a serious charge.

The Etruscan Heritage of Rome

The Etruscans were skilled engineers, and they left a significant heritage in Roman architecture. The Colosseum, aqueducts, and other buildings were possible thanks to the design knowledge the Etruscans taught the Romans. They made the city cleaner and safer: "One example of the Etruscan impact on early Rome was the *cuniculus*, a type of drainage channel that the Etruscans used extensively. Notably, the earliest piece of hydraulic engineering in Rome was a sewer system, the *Cloaca Maxima*" (Howells, 2023, para.11).

The Roman architectural style was significantly influenced by the Etruscans. They adopted the use of what is known as the "Tuscan column," and the earliest monumental buildings in Rome were supposedly commissioned by the Etruscan kings (Howells, 2023).

The Etruscan kings also expanded the arable lands by draining the marshes that filled the valley in the midst of the seven hills. The area would later become the *Forum Romanum*, the beating heart of the Republic and Empire. The Etruscans also improved production capacity and enlarged the city. They built walls around the city to protect the population. They also introduced the gladiatorial contests during the reigns of the Tarquins. This was a funerary practice when a noble or king died. Men were forced to fight to the death, and the bloodshed was a sacrifice to the underworld deities (*How Did the Etruscans Shape Roman History and Society*, n.d.).

Essential Highlights

Like most of its contemporary civilizations, Rome established a monarchy as a political regime. Soon, the young new state created institutions to organize the election of their monarch. Despite the king's absolute power, the Romans developed representative institutions, particularly the Senate, that functioned as a counterbalance for that power. This was an enduring and stable institution throughout all Roman History.

As explained in the previous chapter, the Romans were a mixture of people from different tribes who soon merged to give birth to a unique Roman culture. This blending allowed immigrants and men from conquered tribes to become kings.

Nonetheless, this population was divided regarding its ethnic origin. That division was transferred to the distribution of power and privileges within society. The descendants of the earliest citizens at the time of the founding became the patricians, the class with a higher status and power. The rest of the population were the plebeians, who would play a key role in the next stage of the evolution of the state.

As the last king was expelled and the Roman Kingdom came to an end, the seeds for the next phase in Rome's history were sown. A period where the people would reign supreme and where the ideals of the Republic took root.

.

Part 2: The Republic

(509 B.C.E. - 27 B.C.E.)

.

Chapter 4: The Early Republic

In the aftermath of the monarchy, Rome forged a new identity—one of the people, by the people, for an empire. The last king and the tyranny he established weakened the foundations of the Monarchy, but by then, Rome was a mature political community. The other institutions and the strong tradition of order and hierarchical organization had prepared them to create a new political system that would unleash Rome's greatness.

That political system was the Republic, and it entails a period in Roman history that spans between 509 B.C.E. and 27 B.C.E. It is one of the earliest and most enduring political forms based on popular representation and self-governance. The first two centuries of the Republic are poorly recorded, and most that is known about the period was written by the historian Livy and others from the 1st centuries B.C.E. and C.E. Written history didn't start in Rome until the 3rd century B.C.E.

The early stage of the Republic lasted until 275 B.C.E., when Rome wrested control of southern Italy from Italic natives and Greeks. During this period, Romans fought wars against other Latins, the Etruscans, Gauls, and Samnites, achieving limited unity over the whole territory (*Ancient Rome*—Early Republic, n.d.).

The Structure and Function of the Republican Government

The republican system is based on two main principles. First, the ultimate source of power is the people. The Latin name for this system was *res publica* – literally, public welfare, commonwealth, or (in American terms) a republic. Second, power must be exercised by magistrates who represent popular sovereignty. The arrangement entails a balance of power between different institutions that aims to prevent one from gaining too much control while avoiding stagnation. In modern terms: checks and balances.

The Roman Republic developed a mechanism of control to prevent the return to a monarchy, even in times of crisis. The fundamental principle was collegiality – magistracies had an even number of posts at any given time, with almost no exception. The exercise of power was divided into different functions. There were legislative bodies, executive offices, and magistrates to administer justice. Except for the Senate, magistrates served a specific term in office, usually one year, and there were often restrictions on consecutive terms.

Citizenship in Rome

Citizenship is a key concept for understanding the Roman republican system of representation and popular participation in political affairs. The scope of the concept changed throughout the Republic, but in general terms, full citizenship was restricted to adult men.

Only a full male citizen was considered *optimo jure* (a citizen with the greatest rights): they had full civil and political rights to get married, appear at trial, make an appeal, vote in elections, enter into contracts, and own property. Women were also citizens but didn't have the right to vote or hold public office.

As noted above, Rome's population was divided between patricians (the founders' descendants) and the plebeians (the rest of the people, descendants of immigrants and conquered tribes) and they had different political rights. The Latin word for the entire class of plebeians was the collective singular, *plebs*.

Early in the Republic, intermarriage may have been prohibited, and plebeians faced many restrictions. However, by the mid-Republic, there was political, if not social, equality between the classes. This nominal equality was won after many years of hard-fought struggle.

The Senate

This institution was created almost at the same time as Rome was founded. Originally, it was composed of 100 patricians, direct descendants from the founder families, and their main function during the monarchy was to advise the king and select the candidates to take the throne.

When the Republic was established in 509 B.C.E., the Senate became the advisory council to the two main magistrates that had executive functions, the consuls. The Senate only gathered when these magistrates requested it. However, it was the institution that ensured stability. While the other magistrates had a limited period to hold office, the Senate was life tenure.

Although there are no precise sources, it is believed that during the early Republic, the Senate was composed of 300 members, the *patres et conscripti* ("the fathers and the enrolled"). This suggests not only that the patricians were included but also the plebeians, although the groups remained separate. Even though the Senate didn't have executive power, decisions approved by the Senate were mainly followed by the magistrates and enacted as law (Vermeule et al., 2023). After all, if a consul made enemies in the Senate, what sort of political career could they possibly have after their term in office?

Roman Magistrates

The executive magistrates traditionally followed the *cursus honorum*, a series of offices to which an aspiring Roman could be elected. All of them derived their power from the popular assemblies that elected them, and the terms of office were one year.

The highest office consisted of two consuls. They were the chief executives of the state and commanded the army in war. The consuls were followed by the praetors who administered justice, presided over the courts, and (later) were the commanders of provincial armies.

The aediles managed domestic issues such as the public market or street spectacles. This office may not have been a required step, but it offered Roman politicians an opportunity to impress the Roman people with lavish games and festivals. The electorate remembered them vividly, and electoral success to higher offices often followed noteworthy performances. Finally, the quaestors were accountants for the treasury and frequently served under consuls and praetors in the army to manage logistics.

Several offices existed outside the *cursus honorum*. Plebeians elected 10 tribunes of the plebs each year, who had the power of vetoing any other magistrate's actions. Their bodies were sacrosanct, meaning that anyone who harmed a plebeian tribune could be killed with impunity. An ongoing bone of contention throughout the Republic was the power of the tribunate, with some senators trying to restrict their authority, and others trying to expand it.

The censors served 18-month terms. While in office, they were responsible for conducting the Roman census, appraising the value of every citizen's property, and assigning them to the appropriate economic class. In addition, they controlled the list of senators. They could remove members who did not meet the property qualifications or who failed to uphold traditional Roman values. Finally, the censors often oversaw large public works projects and negotiated contracts on behalf of the state. Elections for the censorship were held once every five years.

Another irregular office was created in 501 B.C.E., the dictator. According to tradition, its main role was to replace the consuls in times of crisis when the circumstances demanded a strong and centralized military command. A dictator lasted in office for six months and was "also termed the master of the army (*magister populi*), and he appointed a subordinate cavalry commander, the master of horses (*magister equitum*)" (Seller et al., 2023). It was a constitutional resource to sustain the system's stability in times of great turmoil. Indeed, some dictators were appointed to ensure the integrity of elections for regular magistracies.

Roman Assemblies

Popular assemblies were the cornerstone of the whole republican system, as they represented the ability of the *Populus Romanus*, the Roman People as a collective unit, to govern itself. Each citizen was a member of several different assemblies, each organized according to how the people would meet to perform a given function.

The Curiate Assembly

The *comitia curiata* dates back to the Monarchy. There were 30 *curiae*, each representing one of Rome's 30 original patrician families. In the earliest years of the Republic, the Curiate Assembly could pass legislation, try judicial cases, and elect consuls. Since it was originally a patrician assembly, plebeians could not vote in it, but they could participate. Moreover, tribunes of the plebs could veto the decrees of the consul who presided over the Curiate Assembly. Over the course of the Republic, the *comitia curiata* declined in importance, eventually able only to confirm the investment of higher magistrates with *imperium* and ratify wills.

The Centuriate Assembly

The *comitia centuriata* originally divided the citizenry into groups of 100 based on their military role. As Roman society developed distinct economic classes, the determining factor became wealth. This dovetailed nicely with a citizen militia-style army, since the centuries of the highest classes would be the men able to afford the best arms and armor.

During the first half of the Republic, there were 193 centuries. The number increased later to 373. Arranged on the battlefield, they always had an equal paper strength. However, on the electoral field, poorer centuries grew to have more members, and thus the votes of the wealthy carried more weight than the poor. Conversely, the wealthy stood to lose far more resources in the case of a military reverse.

When voting, each century had a single vote. The simple majority within each century determined which way the century as a whole voted. During a vote, the centuries would vote one at a time, starting with the wealthiest. Once a simple majority of centuries voted in a certain direction, the vote was finished. The lowest centuries rarely voted.

The Centuriate Assembly inherited some powers from the Curiate Assembly after the first few decades of the Republic. Ultimately, it elected consuls and praetors and invested them with *imperium*. Likewise, it elected the censors and gave them the power to conduct the census. As the *Populus Romanus* in its military capacity, the *comitia centuriata* was the only instrument of the Roman state able to declare war. Finally, it was the court of final appeal for treason trials.

The Tribal Assembly

The *comitia tributa* represented the Roman people in its tribal capacity. Unlike the Curiate Assembly, where the distinction was ethnic, and the Centuriate Assembly, where it was economic, the Tribal Assembly was geographic. There were 35 Roman tribes – four urban, and 31 rural. They were somewhat analogous to U.S. congressional districts and were just as prone to gerrymandering. Like the Centuriate Assembly, each tribe had one vote, and it was cast according to a simple majority of its members. The Tribal Assembly elected lower magistrates like quaestors and aediles, and it presided over non-capital trials.

Roman Heroes of the Early Republic

The consolidation of a new political system can only be achieved with the participation of large parts of the community. However, any process of change requires leaders to inspire and guide the masses. Later Romans would look back on semi-legendary figures who embodied traditional Roman values as heroes of the Republic. These important figures are closely associated with the emergence of Republican institutions. Several of them remain symbolic of true patriotism to this day. The following figures represent a small sample of Roman heroes from the early Republic.

Agrippa Menenius Lanatus

Menenius was appointed consul of the Republic and had to deal with the plebeians who complained about their lack of rights and impoverished living conditions. In 494 B.C.E., Rome was under enemy attack, and the *plebs* rebelled and walked out of the city, refusing to fight for Rome. Instead, they camped on the Sacred Mount, roughly three miles from the city. The episode became known as the first

"Secession of the Plebs." Menenius took on the mission of negotiating with the rebels and convincing them to rejoin their compatriots.

He prevailed upon the crowd with a fable. The story was about a time when a man's limbs got angry with his belly because they had to work hard for it while the belly didn't do anything for them. The limbs agreed not to work anymore. Since the belly didn't obtain any food or water, the body started to starve, including the limbs. Then, the limbs understood that every part of the body was important for the survival of the whole (*Menenius Agrippa's Fable*, B.C. 494, n.d.).

According to tradition, the fable told by Agrippa Menenius persuaded the plebeians to stop the riot and return to Rome's defense.

Gnaeus Marcius Coriolanus

Coriolanus was a Roman soldier who earned the nickname "Coriolanus" after his distinguished performance during the siege of Corioli (493 B.C.E.). By then, Rome was at war with the Volsci, an Italic tribe to the southeast of Rome. The Volsci launched a sneak attack on Rome to weaken the siege of Corioli. However, Coriolanus led his troops to the gates of Corioli and set fire to the neighboring houses. When news reached the Volscian troops marching on Rome, they turned back in dismay.

However, Coriolanus was later sent into exile because of a dispute with the *plebs*. He went to live among his former enemy, the Volsci, and offered to guide their army against Rome. When he was about to attack his former city, his mother, Veturia, and his wife, Volumnia, were brought to the camp to persuade him to abandon his decision (Britannica Encyclopaedia, 2019). They convinced him to withdraw. In honor of these women, the Romans dedicated a temple to *Fortuna*, goddess of luck and good fortune.

The Gens Fabia

The *Fabii* were one of the ancient patrician families of Rome, and they were the wealthiest and most powerful. Between 485 and 479 B.C.E., a Fabius held the consulship seven consecutive times. At first, they were hated by the plebeians as much as the rest of the patricians, but at one point, one of the Fabian consuls started advocating for plebeian rights. That earned the family the sympathy of the plebeians and the rage of the patricians, who called the *Fabii* traitors.

In 479 B.C.E., Rome was at war with Veii, the most powerful Etruscan city. Kaeso Fabius spoke in front of the Senate on behalf of the whole *gens Fabia* and asked for the honor of confronting the enemies on their own. The Senate accepted, and the following day, the family left the city to camp by the small Cremera River between Rome and Veii. No other patrician family offered to join them.

The entire *gens Fabia* and all of their clients went to the camp at Cremera. They resisted for two years, successfully repelling the Veientines, until one day they were ambushed and destroyed. Of the 306 members of the *Gens Fabia*, only one boy was left alive and returned to Rome (Harding, n.d.). The specifics of the story are legendary, and they closely resemble the last stand of the 300 Spartans at Thermopylae. Moreover, the *gens Fabia* remained one of the most distinguished patrician families of the Roman Republic, so it is unlikely that the 306 *Fabii* at the battle comprised the entire *gens*. Yet the battle may well have occurred, and there is evidence that the *Fabii* held country estates around the Cremera River.

Lucius Quinctius Cincinnatus

In 458, B.C.E., a Roman army was surrounded by enemies on Mount Algidus, and Cincinnatus, a farmer, was appointed dictator by the Senate to save it. Cincinnatus was not the first Roman dictator, but he may have been the most symbolic of the office when performed properly.

Cincinnatus is remembered for having kept the title of dictator only for the 16 days that it took him to save the trapped army and ensure Rome's safety. It is uncertain if his story is real or if it has been adorned by tradition. However, his figure was praised by the Romans because he represented the value of republican institutions above personal ambitions:

"He knew that his duty as a Roman dictator was to ameliorate the situation as quickly as possible. When order had been restored, his job was to allow the state to return to its normal operations—one without a dictator" (Burns, 2022, para. 4).

Verginia

In 454 B.C.E., the Romans elected a board of 10 legislators to help smooth the tensions between patricians and plebeians. Among the *decemviri* or "board of 10" was the powerful patrician Appius Claudius Crassus Inregillensis Sabinus. The board traveled to Athens, seeking inspiration from the law code of the great Athenian lawgiver Solon. They returned, and after two years debates continued over how to compile just legislation.

Verginia was the daughter of a plebeian centurion named Lucius Verginius. She was very beautiful, and in 452 B.C.E., the powerful patrician *decemvir* Appius Claudius wanted to possess her, but the girl was already engaged. Making use of his superior power, Appius Claudius kidnapped the girl and claimed she was, in fact, a slave.

The plebeians were outraged, and Lucius Verginius took a knife and killed his daughter in the public market to save her from such dishonor. The event triggered the "Second Secession of the Plebs" that ended with the overthrow of Appius Claudius and his henchmen and restored Republican values (Virginia, n.d.).

In 449 B.C.E. the Twelve Tables were published based on the work of the *decemviri*. They were Rome's first written laws, defining terms and procedures. Most importantly, they clearly expressed the rights and responsibilities of patricians and plebeians. Ultimately, they did not completely resolve Rome's social problems, but they eased some of the tension between the two major classes. And though they might not constitute a fully articulated law code, the Twelve Tables formed the basis of Roman law until the fall of the Western Empire in C.E. 476.

Appius Claudius Caecus

Appius Claudius was a member of the patrician class, appointed censor in 312 B.C.E. During his censorship, he started a series of reforms to allow sons of freedmen into the Senate and other measures to improve land distribution among the lower classes. This earned him the resentment of the other patricians and he was accused of being a demagogue who only launched those reforms to gain popular support and concentrate power.

Nonetheless, his most important legacy was the many building projects he carried out during his mandate. The most remarkable were the *Aqua Appia*, the first aqueduct in Rome that brought water to the city, and the Appian Way, or *Via Appia*. It was the first road used to transport military supplies across Italy and enable trade between Rome and

Capua, an important city in southern Italy. It originally ran the 132 miles to Capua, but it was extended to 230 miles over many years, eventually connecting Rome with Brundisium, an important port on the heel of Italy's boot (Hoffman, n.d.).

The Struggle of the Orders

As explained, Roman society was divided into patricians and plebeians based on their ethnic origin, which was linked to the foundation of Rome. They had significant differences regarding civil and political rights. This distinction wasn't supported by a legal frame but by tradition, status, and mutual recognition as the founders' descendants or later immigrants.

Status was the main factor that determined the hierarchical organization of Roman society (*The Struggle of the Orders: Plebeians and Patricians,* 2016). The strength of tradition in shaping every aspect of daily life and social order created a stable system that survived almost unchanged for nearly four centuries. During the Monarchy and the early Republic, there were some reforms to extend plebeians' rights and access to high magistracies, but the essence of the system prevailed.

Even though the division wasn't based on economic criteria, patrician families were generally wealthier and more powerful than plebeians. The patricians were the nobility, while the plebeians were the farmers and workers of the lower classes. Both classes were considered citizens and could own lands and slaves.

Eventually, the differences in economic and political rights incited a conflict within the Republic: The Struggle of the Orders. The tension boiled over in 494 B.C.E., with the first secession of the plebs, and spanned until 287 B.C.E. During the 200 years of social friction, some wealthy members of the plebeian class reached higher office, gaining them entrance into the Senate. This allied them with the patricians. The nobility of Rome, defined by having an ancestor who had held high office in the family tree, now extended to certain wealthy plebeian families.

However, although some plebeians became even wealthier than many of their patrician counterparts, the vast majority of the population remained poor farmers and laborers, nearly all of them plebeians. Their demands were for structural changes in the legal framework of the Republic. Even after they received legal equality, the tensions between the urban poor and the nobility contributed to the growing difficulty of the republican system to govern a growing empire effectively (*The Struggle of the Orders: Plebeians Unite to Lift their Shackles*, n.d.).

The Twelve Tables

The stories of Menenius and Verginia above developed out of the early Struggle of the Orders. Appius Claudius Crassus was one of ten men appointed to compile the basic laws that would define and ensure the civil rights of Roman society. It was the Romans' first attempt to solve the conflict between the classes. After the overthrow of the last king, the imbalance of powers led to the plebeian secession to the Sacred Mount, leaving the aristocracy without the productive class and the bulk of the army. Therefore, the patricians searched for a peaceful way to solve the conflict (Kershaw, 2023).

Whether Menenius' fable or Verginia's heinous murder are true is debatable. Beyond debate is the existence of the Twelve Tables. The document, first carved on wood and later copper, is the earliest source of Roman written law and the most ancient evidence of written legislation defining a republican form of government (Kershaw, 2023). The laws of the

Twelve Tables set the basis of civil equality in Rome, a civilizational value that endures in contemporary Western societies. This principle implies that all citizens must be treated equally under the law, even those in power.

Written and public laws are the foundations of the republican system, along with periodical and elective public magistrates. The Twelve Tables were placed in the middle of the city, where every citizen could read them.

Before the Twelve Tables, the patricians held political and religious power to create and modify the rules and to interpret and enforce them. As religious authorities, the priests (known as pontifices), played a role in judicial procedures. Therefore, the plebeians were at their mercy. The Twelve Tables prevented the abuse of power by the aristocracy and made every citizen aware of their civil rights (Kershaw, 2023).

Before the Twelve Tables, the plebeians only had the tribunes of the plebs as magistrates to represent them in front of the patricians. The legal system was shaped by a patriarchal and patrilineal society, and the conflicts between parties were solved by the *paterfamilias* in any family, whether they were plebeians or patricians. But if it was a major issue, the conflict fell under the jurisdiction of the patrician pontifices. Plebeians were always under the influence or protection of a patrician family, and it was ultimately the latter who decided upon the conflicts.

Some of the major subjects addressed by the Twelve Tables were:

- A pre-established procedure to conduct a trial.
- Common sentences and punishments.
- The rights of the *patresfamilias* regarding inheritance through the masculine line and the right to divorce their wives. It was also allowed to euthanize disabled children, similar to the Spartan system.
- Women's restrictive rights and their conceptualization as citizens with similar rights to minors.
- Property ownership.
- The prohibition of capital punishment without a trial.
- Religious law and burial procedures.
- The prohibition of marriage between members of different orders.

The Struggle of the Orders brought profound changes to the Republic; however, even after the conflict subsided, its embers helped stoke the fire of civil wars that would end with the decline of the Republic.

Roman Expansion in Italy

The early expansion of Rome began almost immediately after its foundation. Romulus and the other warrior kings fought against the neighboring tribes to incorporate the population into the new state and conquer territories to expand the arable lands. By the 6th century B.C.E., the Etruscan kings controlled the Latin communities that lived to the south of the Tiber River.

In 509 B.C.E., Rome centered into a treaty with the city-state of Carthage (present-day Tunisia). Rome accepted Carthage's commercial monopoly across the Mediterranean in exchange for continued Carthaginian hostility toward Rome's Greek and Etruscan adversaries. Carthage sought to prevent Rome from expanding into Sicily and North Africa (Kinder & Hilgemann, 1996).

When the last Etruscan king fell, Rome's hegemony was weakened, and the villages that occupied the region of Latium rebelled against the city. Their alliance, which Rome had dominated during the Monarchy, was called the Latin League, and the Latin War unfolded between 498 and 493 B.C.E. (Kinder & Hilgemann, 1996). Rome fought and defeated its neighbors in the battle of Lake Regillus in 496. Legend holds that the twin gods Castor and Pollux aided the patrician cavalry in the battle, inspiring them to victory. Rome and the Latin League signed the treaty of Cassius in 494 B.C.E.

This treaty not only put the war to an end but also ensured the Latin cities' autonomy, although the treaty set Rome itself as equal to the entire rest of the League. It was a defensive alliance, but any forces raised against external adversaries would fall under Roman control. This system of Rome calling upon the manpower of neighbors and former adversaries allowed a single city-state to punch far above its weight, militarily. And the arrangement had significant consequences for Italy and beyond as the Republic matured.

Both sides conquered territory and founded joint Latin colonies. The treaty ensured the same rights and obligations for all citizens and established freedom to trade. Nonetheless, the League didn't dissolve as it protected Latium from the attacks of the Aequi and the Volsci.

During the early 4th century, Rome had to resist attacks from the Gauls from the north, who settled in the plains of the Po River. The Gauls were a fearsome foe to the Romans, and a warband led by Brennus swept through northern Italy around 387 B.C.E. The Gauls annihilated a Roman army at the Battle of the Allia, about 10 miles north of Rome. Brennus then plundered the city.

The episode became a great source of shame for the Romans and left a near-permanent imprint on their psychology. We have no definitive knowledge of any previous occupation of Rome by a foreign power, and it would be about 800 years before another foreign army succeeded. Later Roman literature presents an almost complete destruction of the city, similar to the razing of Troy. However, the more likely outcome is that the Romans bought off the barbarian warband after an embarrassing defeat, and slowly regained steam over the next several decades. However, their fear of the Gauls remained a defining characteristic of many foreign policy decisions in the late Republic and early Empire.

The Romans later also allied with the Samnites, people who may have been an offshoot of the earlier Sabine population that had not Romanized under the Monarchy (Kinder & Hilgemann, 1996).

Despite the peace heralded by the Treaty of Cassius, Rome became a threat to the Latin colonies when it resumed expansion after its humiliation by the Gauls. A second Latin War broke out a century and a half after the first, and it ended in disaster for the Latins and their allies. The conflict started in 341 and ended in 338 B.C.E., when Rome conquered some Latin and Volscian cities, and the League was finally dissolved. People from the conquered cities were integrated as Roman citizens of various degrees, and they preserved relative autonomy. The conquered city-states had direct relationships with Rome but not with each other (*Latins*, n.d.).

After the end of the Latin War, the Romans started a colonization campaign beyond the lands of Latium. Latins spread in the colonies throughout the peninsula, and the word "Latin" (*latii*) no longer referred to ethnolinguistic criteria. Rather, it became a legal category that came with some of the rights and privileges of Roman citizenship (*Latins*, n.d.).

Essential Highlights

The Republic replaced the Monarchy after the last tyrannical king was overthrown. The new system attempted to prevent absolute power from being concentrated in one person. It created institutions to enable the balance and control of power. The hierarchical Roman society based on principle was modified by several reforms that ensured more representation and rights for the plebeians. The concept of citizenship as the basis for the whole system evolved and expanded throughout the process.

Having laid its foundation firmly on the Italian Peninsula, the Roman Republic eyed horizons further afield. With growth, however, came both opportunity and challenge.

Chapter 5: Expansion and Conflict

As Rome's territories expanded, so did its internal conflicts, a byproduct of ambition and avarice. The new state grew, as did pressure on a population in need of more resources, and tensions driven by inequality. This forced Rome to expand its territories to solve internal crises, but it also caused new conflicts with its neighbors. The balance of power in the surrounding areas of the Mediterranean Sea changed, with consequences for Rome, its allies, and its enemies.

All these changes directly impacted the internal organization. While the Republic expanded, social changes led to new struggles for wealth and power among the traditional classes and among many new citizens who were integrated as Rome expanded the franchise to neighboring cities. Rome also allowed many conquered city-states to keep their cultures and institutions. The only requirement was to provide Rome with soldiers and military support when needed. Offering the defeated a part of the future victory was a great incentive for Rome's enemies to become its allies (*The Roman Republic*, n.d.).

However, it created a new challenge for the Roman Republic: to build a Roman identity that enabled stability and a sense of belonging. This identity developed loyalty to Rome, which would become a solid basis first for the Republic and later for the greatest empire of antiquity.

The Effects of Rome's Territorial Expansion

The Annexed Territories

Rome was under constant aggression by neighboring tribes and other people who came from outside the peninsula. War was, on occasion, defensive to repel its enemies and, on other occasions, offensive to gain allies and strengthen its position. Roman expansion wasn't a peaceful colonization process. Instead, it was a sequence of wars that eventually provided Rome with the identity needed to strengthen the state.

During the 3rd century B.C.E., the Romans fought and subjugated most of the people living on the Italian peninsula. Their greatest concern was the heavy Greek presence in the South, particularly the vast port of Tarentum. Later, the Romans directed their attention to the Po Valley, the islands of Sardinia and Sicily, and the southern region of Hispania (present-day Spain).

In the early 3rd century B.C.E., the Greeks of Thurii were under constant attack by the Lucani, a southern Italic tribe, and they asked for Rome's military intervention. Tarentum, the most powerful Greek colony in Italy, felt that Thurii should have turned to fellow Greeks instead of the Romans. After all, Roman intervention would increase their influence in the South. In 282 B.C.E., the Romans saved Thurii from a siege by the Lucani, Samnites, and Bruttians, spreading Rome's control farther out from Latium and into Southern Italy. This alerted the Tarentines, who attacked Roman ships near the coast and sacked Thurii. Tarentum took Roman soldiers as prisoners, and in response, Rome declared war.

The Pyrrhic War

Tarentum engaged mainland Greece's participation. King Pyrrhus of Epirus, one of the most remarkable military leaders of the age, commanded a force of Greek mercenaries and invaded Italy from the south in 280 B.C.E. He brought 25,000 soldiers and 20 war elephants, a strategy that would later be used by other enemies of Rome.

Rome's first battle against a sophisticated Hellenistic Greek army did not go well. Pyrrhus quickly defeated them at Heraclea and enlisted the help of the Samnites. The king of Epirus offered peace to Rome, but it entailed confining their influence to central Italy. The now elderly Appius Claudius Caecus (see above, Chapter 4) persuaded the Senate to keep fighting, since peace would be perceived as a weakness if the terms were not favorable to Rome.

Appius' sentiment evoked long-held Roman tradition. Rome was always a patron, never a client.

Roman commanders held *imperium* over their troops – they could, and often did, execute any legionnaire who left his position in the battle line. Moreover, the Roman approach to war differed greatly from that of the city-states in the Hellenistic East. For Rome, it was definitional. The word "peace" essentially meant a favorable treaty for the *Populus Romanus*. A favorable treaty, by definition, was one that relegated the opponent to permanent client status. It was all or nothing – once war started, it did not end until the enemy became a client. In contrast, Hellenistic states would often make peace after a slight gain or loss of treasure or territory and reopen hostilities a few years later to try their luck again. Enemy societies rarely appreciated the misalignment of victory conditions between themselves and the Romans.

Pyrrhus attacked Rome again at Asculum in 279 B.C.E. However, he suffered many casualties against the ferocious legionnaires. Our sources conflict on who actually won the battle – both sides suffered significant losses. According to Plutarch, who claimed that Pyrrhus came away victorious, the king of Epirus felt that "another such [victory] would utterly undo him." His successes against an implacable Rome coined the expression "Pyrrhic Victory," any win purchased at too high a cost (Badian et al., 2023, para. 13). Just one year after the loss at Heraclea, Rome fought Pyrrhus to a standstill.

Pyrrhus left Italy to fight against the Carthaginians in Sicily. In 275 B.C.E., he returned and attacked Rome again, but this time, the Romans defeated him at the battle of Beneventum. This was a key victory for Rome not only because it proved the power of its army to repel a foreign invasion and control the tribes in Southern Italy, but because it validated the Roman system against a powerful opponent. The Pyrrhic War illustrated that Rome's arrangement with its allies could allow a single city-state to draw upon the manpower reserves of an entire geographic region. This meant that Roman forces could sustain horrific losses and keep fighting when any other society would have capitulated long before.

The Punic Wars

Carthage was a 9th century B.C.E. colony of the Phoenician city Tyre, in modern Lebanon. The Phoenicians founded several trade colonies in the Western Mediterranean in the early 1st millennium B.C.E., and Carthage was well-positioned on the coast of modern Tunisia. In time, Carthage grew into an independent city-state, and then a mercantile empire that dominated trade in the Western Mediterranean. Rome's expansion proved a threat, and diplomatic relations ran hot and cold from the very founding of the Republic in 509 B.C.E.

The conflicts reached their peak during the 3rd century B.C.E., in the three Punic Wars. *Punicus* was the Latin adjective for "Phoenician." For Rome, Carthage was a threat to Roman hegemony on the peninsula due to its alliances with rebel tribes and its presence in nearby Sicily. The first objective Rome pursued was to limit Carthaginian influence on the peninsula, but the Carthaginian Empire sought to hamper the growth of a city-state it considered an upstart.

The First Punic War

The First Punic War (264–241 B.C.E.) started after the eruption of a military and diplomatic conflict in Sicily. About 288 B.C.E., a roving band of Italic mercenaries took over the port of Messina in the northeast corner of the island. It sat opposite Rhegium on the toe of Italy's boot, and the two cities controlled the crossing from the island to the mainland. The mercenary group called itself the Mamertines after Mamers, an Italic war god. For 20 years they raided and plundered the areas around Messina.

Eventually, in 264 B.C.E., King Hiero II of Syracuse moved to destroy them, but the Mamertines appealed to Carthage for help. A Carthaginian fleet arrived to help, and the Syracusans withdrew, but the Mamertines soon chafed under Carthaginian control – they now appealed to Rome. The Romans had misgivings about helping a mercenary group that had unjustly conquered a city, but they feared Carthaginian proximity to Italy even more. grew worried about Carthaginian proximity to Italy. Rome allied itself to the Mamertines, and Syracuse to

Carthage. The defining wars of the Republic had begun.

Rome sent an army of 40,000 to Sicily. The Romans quickly subdued Syracuse, which received no aid from Carthage. The Syracusans were forced to agree to supply Roman troops in the Sicilian theater. Although a great naval power, the Carthaginians did not feel confident about engaging such a large Roman force on the rugged Sicilian terrain. Nevertheless, they recruited a mercenary army of over 50,000 infantry, including warriors from African tribes, Iberians from Spain, and Celts from France and Britain. The ground war in Sicily was a slog, but the Romans generally outperformed Carthage.

But Carthage ruled the seas and was able to supply its forces in Sicily and raid the Italian coastline with impunity. The ground war became a stalemate. Rome had never engaged in large-scale naval warfare, but it needed to hit Carthage where it hurt. Exhibiting the Roman tendency to absorb rather than exclude, the Romans built a fleet using a wrecked Carthaginian warship as a model. Of course, the inexperienced Roman crews were no match for their opponents, which they learned in several small engagements. The Carthaginian ships were too maneuverable and could easily ram and sink the Roman vessels.

However, the Romans developed a device they called the *corvus* or "raven." It was a movable gangplank with a spike on the end that, when dropped, would penetrate the deck of the opposing ship, building an immovable bridge from one ship to another. A handful of heavily armed Roman marines could overwhelm the lightly defended Carthaginian sailors. At the Battle of Mylae in 260 B.C.E., the *corvus* helped the Romans overcome a large Carthaginian fleet.

The Romans now felt confident enough in their navy to press Carthage. They brought together considerable resources to assemble a fleet of over 300 warships with many more transports and ancillary vessels. Aboard the transports was an invasion force of 26,000 veteran soldiers. They planned to invade Carthage itself. However, the Carthaginians assembled their entire navy to defend the homeland, and the forces met off Cape Ecnomus in southern Sicily in 256 B.C.E. Scholars debate whether it is the largest naval battle in human history, but largest or not, the resources of human and material capital spent are staggering – perhaps 50,000 men killed, and 50 ships sunk in a single engagement.

The Roman invasion of Africa was only partially successful. The Romans defeated Carthage in 255 B.C.E., but they tried to impose terms so harsh that the Carthaginians soon regained their will to fight. They pushed the Romans back, but the fleet sent to evacuate the legions from Africa defeated another Carthaginian fleet at the Battle of Cape Hermaeum. But the entire successful Roman fleet was sunk in a violent storm off the south coast of Sicily. The losses may have exceeded 100,000 soldiers and crewmen and 350 warships.

Yet the Roman system could withstand such staggering losses and continue. They built and crewed another fleet quickly, renewing the war in Sicily. But it dragged on, with the Romans winning some victories on land and at sea, but the Carthaginians holding their own in Sicily under the leadership of General Hamilcar Barca. In 253 B.C.E., the Romans lost another fleet of 150 ships in a massive storm.

The toll on both great civilizations continued to rise, with the Carthaginians seeking massive loans from Egypt, and Roman nobles donating personal finances to the bankrupt state. Eventually, in 241 B.C.E., after 23 years of atrocious bloodshed, the Carthaginians sued for peace. The settlement required Carthage to abandon all its territory in Sicily, Sardinia, and Corsica, and pay massive reparations to Rome to recoup the cost of the war. The Carthaginian Empire in Africa and Spain remained intact. For the next 20 years, Hamilcar Barca would expand Carthaginian territory in Spain. Rome would add Sicily to the *Imperium Romanum* as the first province outside the Italian peninsula. Corsica and Sardinia soon followed. To govern these provinces, the Senate would appoint a praetor who had just finished his term of office. Such a governor was called a propraetor.

The Second Punic War

Despite the victory and peace treaty, Rome was determined to destroy the Carthaginian Empire and prepared a double attack on Spain and Africa, departing from Sicily. However, those plans were delayed due to the emergence of a new military leader, Hannibal Barca, son of Hamilcar Barca. The hero of the first Punic War had ruled Hispania like a private kingdom, and after Hamilcar's death in 228 B.C.E., Hannibal grew in influence.

Hannibal planned to attack Rome directly. Instead of reaching through the south or from the islands, which were predictable moves and guarded by the now-dominant Roman fleet, he outlined a bold plan. He would reach Rome from the north. He gathered an army of 50,000 men, including many native Iberians, and 9,000 cavalry. He included 37 elephants on his trek across the Pyrenees and the Alps.

The Romans had no defensive positions in the Alps and didn't expect an attack from the north, so Hannibal reached the Po Valley in 218 B.C.E., counting on the support of the Gauls. After the first victories, Hannibal consolidated his position in the north but decided not to attack Rome directly until he could erode support from its allies.

The Roman legions confronted Hannibal's army on the battlefield several times and suffered repeated disasters – Trebia in 218 and Lake Trasimene in 217. The Battle of Cannae in 216 B.C.E. was the worst. An army of over 80,000 Romans and allies was almost completely annihilated by an inferior force of 50,000. Hannibal employed the first well-attested double envelopment or "pincer" attack in Western warfare to devastating effect.

Hannibal was able to hold his position and extend his influence across much of Italy, but it was difficult to obtain supplies, manage allies and mercenaries of many different ethnicities, and keep his army loyal. The fact that he managed to do so while sitting in enemy territory for 14 years places him among the greatest strategic and logistic generals in history.

On the other side, Rome struggled to repel an invader of such genius, but the same system that absorbed catastrophic losses in the previous generation managed to field enough men to keep the Carthaginian terror away from the walls of Rome. Moreover, they conducted the war in several theaters, including Spain and, in 204, Africa itself.

By 203 B.C.E., the Romans had long known not to attack Hannibal head-on. Instead, they maneuvered in a strategic dance to take and defend strongholds and threaten supply lines. At that point, with the brilliant Roman general Publius Cornelius Scipio Africanus devastating the African countryside, the Carthaginian Senate recalled their greatest general, and Hannibal withdrew back to Africa.

In 202 B.C.E., Hannibal confronted the Romans in the Battle of Zama. The Romans, led by Scipio, fielded 30,000 men, many of the survivors of the disaster at Cannae 14 years before. He received help from Masinissa, a Numidian king who had defected from the Carthaginians. Hannibal commanded a force of 50,000, including 80 war elephants. The Romans won a terribly hard-fought but complete victory that "effectively ended both Hannibal's command of Carthaginian forces and also Carthage's chances to significantly oppose Rome" (Hunt, 2018, para. 1). The Carthaginian Senate exiled Hannibal and sued for peace. They lost all their overseas territory, some of their African territory, and had to pay Rome a massive amount in reparations. Most importantly, the treaty stipulated that Carthage could not wage war without Rome's permission.

The Third Punic War

Despite the success in the battle of Zama, many Romans felt the Carthaginian threat was not gone. Cato the Elder and other prominent senators advocated for war. In 149 B.C.E., the Roman Senate secured a good reason to attack Carthage, when the latter attacked Numidia, still led by a now elderly Masinissa, who was mercilessly raiding Carthaginian territory. He knew the Romans would intervene if Carthage retaliated (The Punic Wars vs. Carthage, n.d.).

Rome prepared its troops to besiege Carthage, but with no positive outcomes for two years. Eventually, in 146, a new military leader entered the scene: Scipio Aemilianus. He succeeded in successfully blockading Carthage itself. Scipio's army breached the walls and captured the city house by house until 50,000 Carthaginian people surrendered. The city was destroyed, and the survivors were sold as slaves. The Carthaginian Empire had disappeared, and it became the Roman province of Africa (Ray, 2023). However, the Romans left the city empty for the next century, when they rebuilt it as a Roman colony.

The Macedonian and Seleucid Wars

The fact that Rome could field (and lose) massive armies time and time again through the 3rd century B.C.E. while fighting Carthage is noteworthy. But the Romans also operated in other theaters against other opponents at the same time. The struggles between Rome and several Hellenistic Greek states are known as the Macedonian Wars. Four conflicts during the 3rd and 2nd centuries B.C.E. spread Rome's influence in the East.

By 214 B.C.E., the successors of Alexander the Great's empire had been fighting one another for over a century. The three major players were Antigonid Macedonia, Ptolemaic Egypt, and the Seleucid Empire from the Middle East to India. Under the rule of Philip V, the Macedonian Empire was a threat to Rome since it had allied with Hannibal. The Macedonian Wars took place in the context of the Punic Wars. Therefore, Rome sought allies among various leagues of Hellenistic Greek city-states primarily to stop Philip from sending aid to Hannibal in Italy. They were successful in doing so.

After the Second Punic War ended, the Romans were fairly disinterested in Greek affairs. However, when tensions between the three great Hellenistic empires flared and threatened to impact the free leagues of Greek city-states, they had nowhere to turn but Rome for help – diplomatic or otherwise. As happened so often in Roman history, once the Greek cities became clients of Rome in 200 B.C.E., the Romans took their job of patron seriously.

Over the following decades, Rome sought to stabilize the political atmosphere in the East. Roman and allied forces defeated Macedonian armies in Greece at Cynoscephalae in 197 B.C.E. and at Pydna in 168. These victories illustrated the superiority of the versatile Roman legions over the inflexible (but nearly unstoppable) Macedonian phalanx. They also ended Macedonia as an independent entity – the Romans divided it into four client states.

Almost simultaneously, the Romans entered into conflict with the vast Seleucid Empire, entering Asia for the first time. Antiochus III ruled the territory from modern Turkey to the Hindu Kush mountains. Nevertheless, Lucius Cornelius Scipio Asiaticus, the younger brother of Hannibal's nemesis Scipio Africanus, smashed Antiochus' superior force at Magnesia in 190. The Romans withdrew, but relieved Antiochus of all his territory in Europe (Chaliakopoulos, 2022). The Seleucid Empire dwindled over the next century until, eventually, its last few cities in Syria fell to Gnaeus Pompeius Magnus in 63 B.C.E.

In the meantime, Rome wrestled with the unruly Macedonians and Greek city-states to maintain peace. After the Romans defeated a Macedonian uprising at a second Battle of Pydna in 148 B.C.E., a league of Greek city-states declared war on Rome. As former allies, the Romans perceived this as a client refusing to meet their obligations. The Romans utterly destroyed Corinth, one of the most culturally advanced city-states in Greece. In the same year that Rome destroyed its greatest enemy, Carthage, it brutally subdued Greece. The Romans plundered all treasure and artistic works from Corinth, and turned Macedonia and Greece into the new provinces of Epirus and Achaea (Kinder & Hilgemann, 1996).

Rome in the West: Expansion in Europe

After the war against Hannibal ended in 202 B.C.E., the Romans also operated widely in the north of Italy and Spain. There, Carthage allied with the tribes that resisted Roman influence, such as the Boii, the Insubres, and the Gallic tribes in the Po Valley. The Gauls, who came from present-day France, joined forces with the Ligurians and attacked the Latin colony of Placentia in 198 B.C.E. However, by 197, the Romans had pacified the entire

Mediterranean coast of Spain, dividing it into two new provinces, Nearer and Further Spain.

The Republic also fought many battles against the Gauls living both north and south of the Alps, and by the end of the period, Rome conquered some of their lands. In 194 B.C.E., Lucius Valerius Flaccus launched a campaign that consolidated Roman hegemony in Italy after defeating the Insubres and the Boii. Peace was established and the Romans built new colonies at Bononia and Aquileia (Saller et al., 2023).

The Romans also built a new road, the *Via Emilia,* to establish trading connections with the northern tribes of Europe. It implied an expansion of the Roman commercial scope. The French territory near the Mediterranean became the Roman province of Gallia Narbonensis in 121 B.C.E., with its capital at modern Narbonne. (*The Roman Republic*, n.d.).

Structural Changes in the High Republic

Impact on Citizenship and a New Balance of Political Power

The role of citizenship was key throughout the whole history of Rome, from the earliest moment of its foundation. The status and rights encompassed in Roman citizenship were progressively transformed and reached more people. During the first stages of expansion, citizenship was framed by land, military service, and political levels of participation: "Because a person had to be physically present in Rome to vote, the extension of voting rights beyond the population of the city itself did not drastically alter the political situation in Rome" (*The Roman Republic*, n.d., para. 13).

After the expansion, there were three types of citizens in Rome (Kinder & Hilgemann, 1996):

- Citizens of the city and the surrounding rural areas. This category included civil and political rights which meant that they could own land and also take part in assemblies and vote. They were the *cives optimo jure*, citizens with full rights.
- Communities with citizenship rights: usually conquered populations who were considered Roman citizens but lacked voting rights at Rome (*civitates sine suffragio*).
- Confederates: These were autonomous city-states that recognized Rome's hegemony – clients, essentially. These cities were *civitates foederatae*, allied states. Their citizens could trade with Rome and even marry full Roman citizens.

It was important for Rome to build a stable and balanced relationship with the new populations and simultaneously avoid risking internal stability. Rome needed soldiers and military support, but that couldn't be achieved without making them part of the political unit. It is difficult to measure how much power should be allowed to a conquered city-state. It had to be enough to develop loyalty to Rome but not so excessive as to hamper Roman hegemony. The right to vote was the main feature that regulated that participation: "The offer of citizenship did help to build a sense of shared identity around loyalty to Rome" (*The Roman Republic*, n.d., para. 13).

Political Organization of the New Territories

Wars cost money and demand resources. Mobilizing an army wasn't an easy task. Since soldiers were Roman citizens, sending troops away on a long military campaign entailed preventing them from working their lands and producing food. Once victory was ensured, there was a second task to address: keeping power. However, relying solely on military forces would be excessively costly for the state, even threatening the food supply.

By the end of the 3rd century B.C.E., the territory of the Roman Republic was nearly 50,200 square miles, and it was inhabited by about 292,000 citizens (Kinder & Hilgemann, 1996). The enlarged territory and population demanded effective political organization and administration. The Republic created formal provinces: "In 241 Sicily became Rome's first province, followed by Sardinia-Corsica in 238, and Spain, divided into two provinces, in 197. After a 50-year hiatus, Macedonia and Africa were annexed in 146, and the province of Asia (northwestern Turkey) in 133" (Hornblower et al., 2023, para. 10).

The Senate appointed officeholders called governors (usually an ex-consul or praetor), a *quaestor*, and three lieutenants called *legati* to govern a province. Their power was limited to the territory of the province. The Republican government found a balance between giving governors enough power to keep the provinces under control but not so much that it would challenge Rome's central power (*The Roman Republic*, n.d.). However, the relative autonomy of the provinces was a temptation for governors who, far away from Rome, abused their power over the provinces' inhabitants to enrich themselves (Encyclopedia Britannica, 2023).

Economic Changes in the Republic

Economic evolution facilitated territorial expansion and simultaneously led to an even greater expansion. Besides the increase in population and, therefore, their military forces, the Republic enlarged its vast network of roads. This made the transportation of goods, weapons, and soldiers easier and safer.

Pacifying the surrounding city-states allowed Rome to expand its arable lands, and that led to an increase in overall production capacity. After conquering more lands and communities, Rome's public finances gained new sources of income. The Republic established two types of taxes: war taxes (*tributum*), and indirect taxes linked to trading (*portoria*, or customs) (Kinder & Hilgemann, 1996).

Higher incomes spread the demand for greater supplies produced in the field. The production rose but also diversified. With the annexation of territory, some upper-class Romans obtained large plantations called *latifundia* to cultivate crops and grow livestock, not only for survival as in the earliest stages of the state, but also for high profit. Many farmers stopped producing grains to dedicate their lands to producing high-value crops like olives and grapes for wine. This process deepened the social division between the classes since those changes were only available for large farms, and the new goods were destined for high-class consumers.

This led to the evolution of trading within the Roman territory and with people beyond its borders. The defeat of the Gauls in the North and the building of the *Via Emilia* enabled trading with Northern Europe. And after the annexation of the Macedonian Empire the Roman marketplace became the entire Mediterranean world. The basis of the Roman economy was agriculture, but trading also gained importance. It led to the development of currency to facilitate the trading of different goods with different cultures in regions outside Roman territories. The Romans started minting coins of copper and alloys until, in 296 B.C.E., they established silver coins (Kinder & Hilgemann, 1996).

The Role of Slavery

The evil of slavery was ubiquitous in the ancient world. A slave wasn't considered a person but property and, therefore, could be sold and bought. According to the law, a slave was defined as a *res* (thing). Even though they lacked most of the common rights free people enjoyed, they had a few to preserve their lives. Slaves remained in the same condition for the rest of their lives, and that place within society was inherited by their offspring.

Many societies allowed slavery, but not all of them developed slavery as the basis of production. Rome's Monarchy is an example of this – Romans employed slaves when they could get them, either in domestic or agricultural service. Acquiring slaves was another element of social status. On the other hand, the massive influx of slaves and new citizens during the Republic meant that slaves became the dominant workforce (Hellie, 2023). Moreover, the inclusion of highly cultured Greek slaves meant that wealthy Romans could outsource education, medicine, engineering, and many other fields to slave labor.

Before the 3rd century B.C.E., slavery wasn't widespread. The increase of slaves in Rome coincides with the years of the greatest expansion of the territories of the Republic: "In 225 B.C., there were an estimated 600,000 slaves in Roman Italy, but only 194 years later that number grew to approximately two million" (Burks, 2008. p. 9).

Unlike more recent civilizations, slavery in Rome (and throughout most of human history) wasn't based on ethnic or racial differences. Instead, stronger populations enslaved vulnerable ones, while trying not to become vulnerable themselves. Greeks enslaved as many Greeks as they did others, likewise with Romans, Africans, Asians, and Middle Easterners. In Rome, slaves "include prisoners of war, sailors captured and sold by pirates, or slaves bought outside Roman territory. In hard times, it was not uncommon for desperate Roman citizens to raise money by selling their children into slavery" (PBS, n.d., para. 3).

The war on the borders of the state was one of the most important sources of slaves because prices were lower. Kidnapping was another common way to take slaves to sell them in the Roman market.

Slaves worked everywhere: On farms, mines, factories, as domestic service in the houses of the *paterfamilias*, and even on public works. Beside them, free people also worked in the Roman system. However, the great expansion of the Republic's citizen population created a huge demand for production that only an equal increase in available slave labor could meet.

Internal Conflict and Social Change

The development of the *latifundia* and the increase in the number of slaves widened the gulf between the rich and poor. Only the wealthiest families could hope to obtain a *latifundium* and dedicate their lands to high-value crops. So, the wealthy were the ones who benefited the most from imperial expansion and the changes it brought.

On the other hand, the massive arrival of slaves to work on the large farms displaced most of the free labor. It was less costly to have slaves; they produced more, and purchasing them was an investment.

Rome struggled to integrate the conquered population, expand public finance, and keep a delicate balance of power. The system that governed a city-state failed to find equilibrium in the economic and demographic growth of an empire. All these changes and their consequences led to social unrest

– the free urban poor resented the wealthy and the slaves; the slaves wanted freedom. Between 132 and 103 B.C.E., two slave wars, also called Servile Wars, further destabilized the system.

Riots happened in Sicily, where there was a higher concentration of slaves. These lands were obtained in the war with Carthage and given to wealthy landowners. The slaves' living conditions were often much worse in greater *latifundia*.

The first riot was led by a slave named Eunus, who organized guerilla tactics to confront the Roman army sent to suppress him. Some slaves escaped or roamed the countryside, stealing what they could to survive. The second followed the same strategy, and although it spanned a few years, it was beaten by the Roman forces.

However, some Republican visionary leaders attempted to make reforms by enacting laws that could prevent the runaway disparity between rich and poor from growing further. Two of them were the Gracchus brothers, both elected as plebeian tribunes.

Tiberius Gracchus' reforms didn't attempt to destroy private property. Instead, he proposed to establish a limit for a *latifundium*, which was already legally set at 500 *iugera* (309 acres). Gracchus suggested that land over the limit should be redistributed to landless citizens to ensure their survival (Ferguson et al., 2023).

His proposition had wide support in the Plebeian Assembly, a subset of the Tribal Assembly without the participation of patricians. However, it was strongly resisted in the Senate, which was mainly composed of large landowners of both classes. The following year, Tiberius tried to be re-elected as Tribune, which was beyond the constitution, although he had enough votes. The election unleashed a violent conflict in the Senate, and Tiberius was killed (Gill, 2019). This was a momentous introduction of violence into the Roman political system.

Ten years later, Gaius Gracchus took Tiberius' place and continued with similar proposals for land reform. In 123 B.C.E., a plague ravaged the crops in the south of Italy, and Gaius ordered the construction of state granaries to ensure food supplies for the entire population. He tried to found colonies in Sicily and Carthage, and humanized laws regarding military conscription. He also advocated for full Roman citizenship for everyone in Italy.

Like Tiberius, Gaius had the common people's support but the Senate's opposition. Violence broke out again, this time with Gaius' supporters killing an opponent. The Senate immediately convened and issued a new type of senatorial decree – the *senatus consultum ultimum*, or ultimate decree of the Senate. It gave the presiding consuls permission to preserve the state by any means necessary, even in violation of civil rights. It was a last-ditch measure to quell political and social tension by force, and its introduction was the most visible institutional symptom of an ailing Republic. Gaius knew he was doomed like his brother, and he committed suicide by falling on the sword of a slave. After his death, the Senate ordered the execution of many of Gaius' supporters and the confiscation of their property (Gill, 2019). The Senate asserted control, but the quickly growing free population of Rome was becoming more disaffected, and more likely to be roused by strong politicians taking a populist approach.

Essential Highlights

In the 3rd and 2nd centuries B.C.E., Roman territory expanded and dominated much of Western Europe, Northern Africa, and the ruins of the Macedonian Empire in Greece and Asia Minor. Through several wars, . Rome consolidated its supremacy over the Mediterranean Sea and the surrounding areas. This expansion was enabled by economic and political evolution, and at the same time, the annexation of lands and the acquisition of slaves triggered a large-scale strain on Republican institutions.

As a counterpart, all these changes brought internal conflicts, and the system revealed contradictions and inconsistencies that led Rome down a path of decline for the Republic.

After a string of miraculous successes, it stood unchallenged in its raw might for several centuries. Yet, every entity, no matter how powerful, has its breaking point. The next chapter will explore how, while the power of Rome over its empire grew, the institutions of the Republic would be shaken to dust.

Chapter 6: The Fall of the Republic

In times of war, the law falls silent. –Cicero.

The Crisis of the Late Republic

The crisis of the Republic was a consequence of multiple causes that evolved and remained underappreciated for decades. One of them was the hierarchical nature of Roman social organization. It had given stability to the early society and was supported by the strength of tradition, but it became the main source of rampant economic inequalities. The differences between the patricians and the plebeians during the monarchy or even the early

Republic were mainly a matter of status. It certainly manifested in their political rights and the expansion of their wealth, but as there was little to share and a lot of trouble to deal with (external war, for instance), those differences were set aside. Moreover, the patron-client relationship offered protection and stability to many poorer free Romans.

When the Republic expanded, there was wealth and land to distribute. On the one hand, it was used to encourage people to support military campaigns, and on the other hand, the rewards weren't equally assigned (*Crises of the Republic*, n.d.). The creation of *latifundia* and the establishment of slaves as the primary workforce led many people (mostly plebeians) to impoverishment. Duncan explains (Boissoneault, 2017, para. 6):

> After Rome conquers Carthage, and after they decide to annex Greece, and after they conquer Spain and acquire all the silver mines, you have wealth on an unprecedented scale coming into Rome. The flood of wealth was making the richest of the rich Romans wealthier.

All that wealth was concentrated in the hands of the senatorial elite, consuls, and generals. Meanwhile, the plebeians were forced to leave their lands to fight for Rome and received very little in return.

Economic inequality and the living conditions of large parts of the plebeian population and the enslaved people led to social unrest. Revolts became more frequent, and the once-essential values of being Roman, such as *fides*, *gravitas*, and *dignitas*, slowly lost meaning for many citizens.

These conflicts didn't boil over every day, and there were several attempts to reduce the turmoil and appease the citizens. These initiatives often repurposed the institutions that encompassed the Republic. They implied building a whole new equilibrium of power and a system of new checks and balances. While the lower classes gained rights, constant crises slowly pushed the government toward centralized power. The Senate's authority diminished while a small number of politicians, many of whom followed a populist agenda, accrued tremendous influence.

The Republic had created the institutions to prevent drastic political changes in times of crisis and to avoid a return to monarchy. However, as the internal conflicts increased and the external threats rose, crises became the norm instead of the exception. Neither the Senate or the assemblies were able to solve people's needs, and that led to the discredit of the state (Boissoneault, 2017).

The Social War

As the Republic reinforced its supremacy in the Mediterranean and subjugated other powers, the policy toward the conquered people also changed. In the past, conquered tribes kept their autonomy and became Roman allies. When the Republic expanded during the 4th and 3rd centuries, these people often sought Roman citizenship to enjoy the benefits of the expansion. However, the growing population of citizens without voting rights became a source of conflict as these people lacked any sense of identity with Rome.

During the expansion phase, Italy was a confederation. Italians had the same economic inequalities as Roman citizens but didn't have the right to vote. A civil war broke out in 90–89 B.C.E. between Rome and the Italian allies or *socii*, hence the term Social War. The Italians organized their confederacy and gathered an army to confront the Roman troops.

The rebels were successful in the North and the South, and to appease the conflict, the Consul Lucius Julius Caesar passed a law to extend Roman citizenship to the Italians. Some tribes, like the Samnites, resisted but were fiercely repressed. However, peace was ensured by establishing new rights for the *socii* and the creation of the municipal organization of the communities as part of the Roman state (Encyclopedia Britannica, 2018).

The Rise of Popular Leaders

The Failure of the Gracchan Reforms

As discussed in the last chapter, Tiberius and Gaius Gracchus had attempted to implement land reform to limit the concentration of land in the hands of the super-rich. As plebeian tribunes, the bills they passed through the Plebeian Assembly carried the force of law, but they had almost no senatorial support. Indeed, both brothers were killed for their efforts to threaten the traditional order (*10000 years of economy*, n.d.).

The general aftermath of Gracchan attempts at reform was negative. The plebeians didn't derive any long-lasting benefit from them, and social unrest increased. In the end, the failure of this attempt contributed to weakening the loyalty of citizens to the state. Until then, in the conflict of interest between individual and collective, the solution always leaned toward the state. The Gracchi posed a disruptive question: "Who was to govern Rome, the Senate or the People?" (Henderson, 1968, p. 1). The Gracchan reforms pushed the Senate to a defensive position in front of the citizens, and that undermined its power and the soul of the Republican system.

The Military in Politics

In times of the monarchy, the army was closely linked to the social organization of Roman society.

One's role in the army was associated with status, and that status was determined by wealth. The lowest groups were excluded from the army and, therefore, lacked rights. If they couldn't afford military equipment, they couldn't be part of the army.

During the Republic, the army was organized into legions. They were the backbone of Roman identity in lands far away from the capital. The sense of belonging to the army was the main source of loyalty to Rome, fighting in distant places for little reward. The generals played a key role in the legions, but it was difficult for the Republic to keep a balance between allowing enough power to control the troops but not enough to challenge central authority.

Things began to change when seasonal campaigns were replaced by lengthy tours of duty, sometimes for years on end. Then, the generals slowly became the patrons of their soldiers, paying them in the form of booty captured from the enemy, since the soldiers could not support their families at home otherwise. The loyalty of the soldiers moved from the state to the commander. In a way, it was a fundamentally Roman reflex, for a client to be loyal to their patron – but it conflicted with the administrative apparatus of a growing empire.

Gaius Marius

As the Republic faced military challenges, more troops were needed. In that context, Gaius Marius was elected consul in 107 B.C.E. He was not a native

Roman, but a man from Arpinum, about 60 miles southeast of Rome. Arpinum had received full citizenship earlier in the century, and Marius pursued a political career as an outsider. He became the first person in his family to become consul, a rarity. The consulship was generally held by the traditional nobility, and they called anyone who joined the consular ranks a *novus homo*, a new man – a term of derision. Nevertheless, Marius introduced several military reforms. He allowed people from the lower classes with no property to enlist in the army. The state provided them with armor and weapons (Lloyd, 2013).

While this was part of a necessary solution to deal with campaigns against African rebels and a massive invasion of Germans into northern Italy, Marius' plan created its own issues. The problem was what to do when soldiers retired. He passed a law that assigned a plot of land to each of his retired soldiers. This created a new source of power used by the generals to manipulate people and increase their political power (White, 2011). Marius ended up being elected consul 7 times, remaining popular among the plebeians for many generations after his death. After Marius, a politician who pursued popular policies to further their career was called a *popularis*.

Sulla's Civil War

Lucius Cornelius Sulla was from an illustrious Roman noble family. Although he was originally one of Marius' lieutenants, he became a staunch defender of the rights of the traditional senatorial class. In this period, politicians who sought to further their careers by endearing themselves to the Senate and traditional nobility were called *optimates*, the "best men." He was a brilliant general who won against the rebels during the Social War.

In 88 B.C.E., he became consul. After a falling out with Marius, Sulla marched on Rome with the army he was preparing for a campaign in Asia. He drove Marius out of Italy and repealed many pieces of *popularis* legislation. This deeply disturbed the vast majority of the population of Rome and Italy. Then, he left for Asia.

Lucius Cornelius Cinna served as consul in 87, and he recalled Marius from exile. Together, they instituted a bloody purge of Sulla's supporters in the Senate, confiscating property, murdering, and driving many into exile. When Marius died of illness, Cinna assumed leadership and monopolized the consulship for the next three years. He enacted some popular social and economic reforms but died in a mutiny in 84 B.C.E. (Encyclopedia Britannica, 2008). Left without a clear leader, many old allies of Marius and Cinna defected to Sulla in fear of repercussions upon his return from Asia. Others allied with rebel Italian bands of Samnites and Lucanians who resented Sulla's victory in the Social War.

Sulla returned to Italy in 84 B.C.E. and fought a bloody campaign to retake Rome. He was victorious at the Battle of the Colline Gate just outside the city in 82. Between 82 and 80, he was appointed dictator in consecutive terms, extending the time he could stay in office.

As a dictator, Sulla introduced a series of reforms, trying to strengthen the power of the Senate and reduce that of the plebeian tribunes. His reforms as a dictator eventually led to the further weakening of the Republic and ignited individual ambitions (White, 2011). Even though Sulla fought to strengthen the nobility, he (much like Marius before him) was the focus of loyalty, not the state. Nevertheless, after enacting his optimate reforms, Sulla laid down his dictatorship and retired to private life until he died in 78 B.C.E.

Pompey, Crassus, Caesar: The First Triumvirate

By the middle of the 1st century, the Republic was plunged into a deep crisis. Violent ambitious figures raised and claimed power for themselves, and the Senate was divided into petty factions. Some, like Sulla, were *optimates*, who advocated for power to reside in the Senate. Others followed Marius and Cinna as *populares* who advocated for the plebeians. First, with Marius, then Sulla, these mentalities held power alternately, but by 60 B.C.E., the *populares* had increased their influence again.

Most of the Senate remained staunchly opposed. Therefore, three powerful *populares* made an informal alliance that historians have called the First Triumvirate.

Pompey the Great

Gnaeus Pompeius Magnus was a military leader who had a remarkable performance in Spain during the Social War and helped overcome the famous slave revolt led by Spartacus from 73 to 71 B.C.E. He also went on a brilliant campaign to Greece and Asia, putting an end to the Seleucid Empire and pacifying the region. He returned to Rome with his troops professing loyalty to him, which alerted the Senate. In addition, the sheer amount of wealth his conquests brought in made him the most successful conqueror in Roman history to that point. The population at large adored him for it.

However, he didn't march on Rome like Sulla. Instead, he shared his reward for the military victories with his soldiers and common people, providing money for public buildings. His popularity continued to rise. However, the main problem was that Pompey had promised the veterans under his command to receive farmlands after their retirement, a measure the Senate denied (*How the First Triumvirate Changed Ancient Rome*, n.d.). In 60 B.C.E., Pompey found himself in need of allies to deliver the promises he had made to his troops.

Crassus

Marcus Licinius Crassus was an ex-Sullan who was rumored to be the wealthiest man in Rome. He came from a wealthy plebeian family and augmented his riches by compelling people to sell their properties at lower prices and forming political connections with important businessmen. Many of them were from the *equites*, the knights. They were traditionally wealthy families who were not part of the nobility – that is, they had enjoyed no success in elections for higher office. Others were tax collectors (*How the First Triumvirate Changed Ancient Rome*, n.d.).

Unlike Pompey, Crassus was not hugely popular – many people remembered he helped Sulla win the Battle of the Colline Gate, but some viewed this as a victory against Rome's enemies, others an assault on popular sovereignty. Nevertheless, Crassus had many clients who had used him as a powerful financier. In this way, he was also a threat to the Senate. In 60 B.C.E., Crassus needed help to assist many of the Roman tax collectors in Asia who were his clients.

Caesar

Gaius Julius Caesar (about whom see more below) cut quite a figure in the Senate. His patrician family traced itself back to the Monarchy, and legend held that the Julii were descended from Aeneas' son Ascanius, whose alternate name was Iulus. Yet, recent generations of the family had worked closely with Gaius Marius, Caesar's uncle, and Cinna, Caesar's father-in-law. 60 B.C.E. was the first year Caesar was eligible to run for the consulship, but he needed money and massive support. Crassus could foot the bill. Pompey and his veterans could all vote.

Caesar and Crassus had worked together for years, but Crassus and Pompey hated each other. To bring Pompey around, Caesar offered his daughter Julia in marriage. She was 17, and Pompey was about 47 – six years older than Caesar. Nevertheless, by all accounts, Julia and Pompey were devoted to one another.

The Failure of the Triumvirate

Thus, the First Triumvirate was created, and in 59 B.C.E. Caesar became consul. In office, he railroaded popular legislation through the Assemblies, making many (admittedly, much-needed) reforms. Caesar knew that his bullying of the Senate could lead to prosecution when he left office. So, he enlisted Pompey and Crassus' help to get him assigned as the governor of the two provinces in Gaul, and Illyricum in modern Albania.

However, the triumvirate didn't last because there were deep differences among the triumvirs. However, Caesar called the others to a Council at Luca in 56 B.C.E. They pooled their resources to get Pompey and Crassus elected consuls for 55, despite rampant mob violence in Rome. Pompey received

Spain for his governorship after his term as consul, and Crassus received Syria (Gray, 2023).

For a while, the agreement worked, but everything changed when Crassus died in 53 B.C.E. in the Battle of Carrhae against the Parthians – a terrible blow to Roman prestige. As a result, Pompey searched for more allies in the Senate in fear of Caesar's growing reputation. Meanwhile, Caesar enlarged his power, and the *Imperium Romanum*, through breathtakingly savage military campaigns in Gaul. That was the end of the Triumvirate (Burns, 2023).

Cicero

Neither a member of the *populares* or *optimates*, Marcus Tullius Cicero was a prominent figure in the late Republic. Like Marius, he was from Arpinum and a new man. He was a remarkable oratorical genius with influence both in the Senate and among the people. He could evoke the audience's emotions, no matter if they were plebeians or patricians. He mastered the art of public speaking and implemented innovative strategies that came to be known as Ciceronian rhetoric (Ferguson & Balsdon, 2023). For many, he represents the greatest public speaker in the history of the West. Moreover, he may also be the greatest of all Latin prose stylists.

He had a brief military career, but he stood out for his performance as a politician. He completed the *cursus honorum* holding office as a quaestor, praetor, consul, and proconsul. He was a strong advocate of the Republic, promoting law and order. Because of his influence in the Senate, Caesar called upon him to join the Triumvirate, but he didn't accept.

He was famous for his loyalty to institutions and laws. However, when he was elected consul for 63 B.C.E., he won the election against Catiline, a powerful and greedy patrician who wanted to pass reforms to benefit himself and hide many crimes that he had committed. After his defeat, Catiline prepared a conspiracy to kill Cicero and several senators. Cicero found out about the conspiracy and arrested five of the conspirators (*Teach Democracy*, n.d.).

When Cicero decided to execute the conspirators to save the Republic, Caesar advocated against the death penalty. Cicero thereafter admired Caesar's intellect and cultural refinement but always distrusted his ambition. However, the Senate supported Cicero's decision. Catiline died in battle and several conspirators were executed. Cicero was credited with saving the Republic. After Cicero's finest hour, politicians on all sides sought Cicero's support. Even the *optimates* who looked down on him as a new man recognized his influence. Caesar, in particular, wanted Cicero's support, but the orator's heart was given to the traditional values of Rome.

When the civil war between Caesar and Pompey flared up in 49 B.C.E., Cicero joined Pompey, but lamented the civil strife. Later, in 44, he was accused of taking part in the conspiracy to kill Caesar; but he wasn't at the Senate when it occurred. He didn't want the civil strife to continue and promoted a law of amnesty to Caesar's assassins to restore the Republic, but it was too late. The Second Triumvirate ordered his execution in 43, and his head and hands were displayed on the *rostra,* the public place for the speakers in the Roman Forum (Ferguson & Balsdon, 2023).

Caesar's Civil War

Julius Caesar was born on July 12 or 13, 100 B.C.E. His family had deep roots in Roman history, but recent generations had been less influential. He proved himself a dashing military officer in his youth, winning the Civic Crown at the Siege of Mytilene on the Greek island of Lesbos in 81. The prestigious award was given to a Roman who saved the life of a fellow citizen in battle. He returned to Rome and established himself as a brilliant speaker – second only to Cicero. He was also a successful governor of Further Spain in 61, subduing native tribes and expanding Roman (and his own) influence.

After allying with Pompey and Crassus, his star rose sharply due to his impressive achievements in the Gallic Wars. The Gauls beyond the Alps had always been a problem for Rome since the time of the Monarchy. In 58 B.C.E., Caesar led a campaign into Gaul to support allied Celtic tribes that lived there and were under attack from Germans who were moving across the Rhine River into modern France.

While pacifying all of Gaul, he consolidated Roman control and became a popular leader among the people, bringing in many more slaves and much treasure to the tottering Republic. Inspired by Sulla, he was determined to use his power within the army to promote his political career. In 50 B.C.E., Caesar marched with his troops to northern Italy and stopped at the Rubicon River, the border of his province and Italy. According to the law, he wasn't allowed to take his army south of the river.

However, he talked to his men and told them that the Senate was after him and that if he was removed from his position, he wouldn't be able to fulfill his promise to give them lands and wealth, which had been customary since Marius' reforms.

His speech was convincing, and his people proved to be loyal to him rather than Rome. In January of 49 B.C.E., he crossed the river and entered Italy as a victorious commander. By then, the Triumvirate had already vanished, and Pompey and part of the Senate had departed for Greece. Pompey felt that the hastily raised legions of Italy stood no chance against Caesar's battle-hardened veterans of eight years. However, Pompey had many clients in Greece and Asia from his time there in the 60s. He hired mercenaries and began to train troops to confront Caesar.

In Rome, Caesar didn't find any opposition to seizing power. The civil war between the two popular leaders had begun. While Pompey was training his army in the East, Caesar left for Spain and confronted

Pompey's many supporters there – clients tied to him since the Social War. After defeating them, Caesar moved to attack Pompey in Greece. When the two armies confronted each other at Pharsalus in 48, Caesar defeated Pompey and scattered his forces. Pompey had been hailed as the greatest commander in Roman history. Caesar beat him in less than two years. Pompey fled to Egypt where he was assassinated. Caesar mopped up remnants of the Pompeian faction in wars in Africa and Spain.

Back in Rome, he had himself appointed dictator and enacted several reforms to widen and consolidate his power. At the same time, he enlarged the Senate, decreased the state debt, sponsored a large building program, broke ground on the *Forum Iulium* adjacent to the Roman Forum, and ordered the reconstruction of Carthage and Corinth. To gain popular support, he gave full rights as Roman citizens to foreigners who lived within the territory of the Republic (Stanfield, n.d.).

In 44 B.C.E., Caesar made one more move beyond the law: he appointed himself as dictator for life and claimed absolute power (Stanfield, n.d.).

Caesar's Assassination: The Ides of March

By 44 B.C.E., little remained of the Republic. During the celebration of Lupercalia, a religious festival, Julius Caesar, "seated in a gilded chair at the front of the *rostra*, publicly refused the diadem of kingship presented to him by (Mark) Antony. He already exercised the power of a dictator, and many regarded the gesture as nothing more than pretense" (*Ides of March: The Death of Caesar*, n.d., para 1).

Despite this gesture of rejecting absolute monarchical power, the senators were already persuaded of Caesar's limitless ambition. He already had full control over the state. He didn't accept a crown as king; he passed decrees sitting on an ivory and gold throne; he established as national festivals the anniversaries of his most important victories; he put under his power priests and Vestal Virgins; and last but not least, he forbade magistrates to oppose any of his orders and decrees (*Ides of March: The Death of Caesar*, n.d.). He didn't hold the title of king, but he was one *de facto*. The Senate started to conspire to get rid of him.

The conspirators called themselves "the liberators," and they plotted the assassination of Caesar before his departure to fight against the Parthians, a growing Empire in the East. Among the conspirators, Cassius and Marcus Brutus were the masterminds behind the plan and the ones who would execute it. Marcus Brutus was a man of Caesar's confidence who was the son of Caesar's longtime lover, Servilia.

The day set for the attack was the Ides of March, the 15th. It was a deadline for settling debts and a day of religious celebrations. That day, Caesar went to the Senate for the last time before his military campaign was set to begin. It was meeting that day, ironically enough, in the Theater of Pompey while the Senate house underwent renovations. Cassius, Brutus, and up to 60 other conspiring senators waited for him. At the given signal, they attacked, stabbing Caesar 23 times.

The seasoned warrior fought back unarmed, but finally succumbed, sinking to the floor at the foot of Pompey's statue and pulling his toga over his head in shame. The scene has been immortalized in literature and film. Shakespeare has him fall after recognizing Brutus and uttering the famous words, "*et tu, Brute?*" – the global expression of betrayal. Suetonius, the Roman biographer suggests he said in Greek, "*kai su, teknon?*" In either case, Caesar's last words heralded the end of the Republic.

Essential Highlights

After centuries of expansion, internal struggles and external threats undermined the Republic. While common people fought to expand their rights and improve their economic lot, the upper classes concentrated more and more power and wealth. The *Imperium Romanum* expanded. Keeping the conquered lands under control presented unbeatable challenges to a government designed to run a city-state. Meanwhile, traditional institutions and values perished due to individual greed and a thirst for personal power.

The Republic, once a beacon of democratic ideals, was overshadowed by the looming silhouette of one-man rule. The age of emperors had arrived.

Part 3: The Roman Empire

(27 B.C.E.—476 C.E.)

Chapter 7: The Rise of the Empire

I found Rome a city of bricks and left it a city of marble. –Augustus.

The greatest empire of antiquity was built on the ruins of the Republic. However, there is a continuity. Many structures of the dead system became the basis of the new one. In this chapter, we are going to explore the audacious journey of Rome's first emperor and the birth of an empire.

The Transition from Republic to Empire

It is difficult to establish exactly when the Roman Republic truly died. However, the turning point was indeed Julius Caesar's assassination. Even though he had already assumed absolute power, a few institutions of the Republic remained. The Senate and the consuls had lost political power over the previous 150 years. However, most military campaigns were still led by the consuls, with a few exceptions. Sulla and Caesar became dictators, but they had led imperial military campaigns as proconsuls and, along with Marius, Pompey, and Crassus, used traditional republican institutions. Of course, they did it to benefit themselves and eventually destroyed the system.

As dictator, Caesar held a legitimate title created by the Republic – he refused to be called king. Even though he ruled as an autocrat, the fact that he used the trappings of republican institutions had consequences. Dictatorship as a republican office meant that there was a time limit. Yes, a powerful tyrant could force others to extend the term, but the power of the dictatorship was not transferable. This left an open question after Caesar's death – who would wield power, and from where would the power be derived?

Caesar was the only one of the 66 dictators in Roman history who was declared dictator for life. While it is unlikely that he would have resigned, his premature death leaves that question unanswered. But the most powerful men in Rome after the assassination rejected the office. (Bellomo, 2022, para. 14):

> The dictatorship as an office was banned by (Mark) Antony, who probably wanted to dissociate himself from the office of dictator. However, it was not forgotten. Augustus was offered the dictatorship in 22, and the reason why he rejected it was that Caesar's heir had found new ways to acquire absolute rulership of the empire.

How did Antony try to accrue power to himself without using the office? And how did Augustus succeed?

The Political Aftermath of Caesar's Assassination

The crisis in the Republic deepened sharply after the assassination of Caesar. The Senate didn't have the power it once held, and people had lost confidence in the institutions. The patrician leaders who feared Caesar had been concerned about the emergence of popular leaders who could concentrate all power by appealing to the masses. By the time of the conspiracy, it was already too late.

Even though there were many other political leaders assassinated in Rome, the Ides of March was the only one that caused a complete shift in the political system, not only because Caesar held a position as a perpetual dictator but because his successor, Octavian, would reshape the state within a short time (*What was the Impact of Julius Caesar's Murder?* 2023).

The conspirators had planned the assassination well but didn't calculate the repercussions. They believed that with Caesar, the problems of the Republic died too. On the contrary, the moments after the crime proved them wrong. After Caesar fell dead at the feet of Pompey's statue, Marcus Brutus went to the Temple of Jupiter to speak to the crowd. He believed people would consider it a heroic act of liberation from a despot, but instead, the crowd was furious at him. The original plan was for the Senate to pass an amnesty law to exonerate the conspirators, but considering the situation of social unrest, they were forced to flee from the city (Wasson, 2016).

The Ides of March left a power vacuum, and many ambitious leaders were ready to claim it. The Senate couldn't fill it because it lacked legitimacy and real power. Instead, two men from Caesar's closest circle claimed to be the legitimate heirs to Caesar's position at the top of the Roman order: Mark Antony, one of Julius Caesar's most important generals, and Gaius Julius Caesar Octavianus, Caesar's grand-nephew and adopted son.

Caesar had a son with Cleopatra, the Pharaoh of Ptolemaic Egypt. His name was Ptolemy Caesar, known as Caesarion, but neither he nor his mother were liked in Rome. Moreover, Roman law did not recognize Caesarion as legitimate. After Caesar's death, they both fled to Egypt. Nobody in Rome considered him a real heir, and Cleopatra would never find enough support to impose him. However, she wouldn't give up on her son's right to a throne. She eventually allied with Mark Antony and lent him Egyptian forces to invade Rome as part of his army.

Mark Antony had been a close ally of Caesar and had the support of many of Caesar's followers. He counted on all his troops to take revenge for Caesar's death and establish himself as preeminent. He tried to assert himself, but he faced fierce opposition from the Senate, which saw in Mark Antony the same threat as in Caesar.

On the other hand, Octavian was ready to take his adopted father's place in power and take vengeance on his killers. At first, he allied with Mark Antony, but their partnership was doomed to failure.

The Second Triumvirate

The Republic would have one last chance to survive with the establishment of a Second

Triumvirate. However, internal conflicts would hamper the last attempt to avoid going back to a monarchical system. The Second Triumvirate was the attempt of Mark Antony, Octavian, and a third ally, Marcus Aemilius Lepidus, to form a government that could bend the Senate. However, each of them brought, along with their troops and strength, their ambitions.

The alliance was unstable from the beginning because Antony and Octavian both believed they had the legitimate right to follow Caesar. The Senate, particularly prominent figures like Cicero, were more worried about Antony as they saw him as a potential tyrant – he was notoriously bloodthirsty. Lepidus was a powerful old ally of Ceasar's who had formal control of several legions in Italy as well as the city. However, he was not as volatile as Antony – he could perhaps be reasoned with. Octavian was 19 years old and had no military or political experience. Therefore, he wasn't considered a threat by the Senate.

The Second Triumvirate arranged legislation to give it the power to make laws and appoint magistrates for a period of five years. They used their power to implement a series of extreme measures (Lendering, 2019; *The Second Triumvirate*, n.d.):

- the execution of 4,700 opponents, including Cicero, some other senators, and wealthy knights – confiscating all their property.

- gave farms to Caesar's veterans from confiscated land.
- declared war against the conspirators and defeated them at the Battle of Philippi.
- introduced measures to reduce the Senate's influence, such as depriving it of the power to appoint magistrates and enact laws independently.

The victory of Philippi in 42 B.C.E. was a landmark moment for the Triumvirate, but soon the differences between the two major leaders increased. After the Triumvirate's victory at Philippi, the three Triumvirs divided their areas of influence: Lepidus ruled in Africa, Antony was appointed to the territories in the East and Egypt, and Octavian remained in Rome, controlling Europe. Internal tensions would erode the Triumvirate for the following 10 years.

In 36, Octavian accused Lepidus of plotting against Rome because he attempted to enlarge his influence in other territories. Lepidus was removed from his office. The stage was set for conflict between Antony and Octavian. The winner would control the whole Mediterranean world.

The Pivotal Battle of Actium

Octavian and Antony first divided the empire into equal parts, but their rivalry increased. Antony had married Octavian's sister, Octavia, in 40, but it didn't help smooth the tensions. Instead, Antony centered his attention on the Egyptian queen Cleopatra, believing her money and troops would help him conquer Rome. His idea was to move the capital to Alexandria – he even gifted Roman territory to her in 34, enraging the Roman populace and further antagonizing Octavian.

Aware of Antony's plan, Octavian played a strategic card. He stirred up public and senatorial opinion against Antony all through 32, arguing that he didn't represent the traditional Roman values and became an ally of foreign countries. However, Octavian framed the conflict as a battle against eastern decadence and meddling - he persuaded the Senate to declare war not on Antony, but on Cleopatra.

In 31 B.C.E., Antony's camp was at Actium, on the western coast of Greece. He had the support of the Egyptian navy led by Cleopatra herself. The couple had 500 ships and 70,000 infantry to offer battle against the Roman army (Encyclopedia Britannica, 2023).

When Octavian arrived in Greece with 400 ships and 80,000 infantry, he landed at Patrae and Corinth, and cut Antony's connection with Egypt (Encyclopedia Britannica, 2023). Antony and Cleopatra were isolated, and the supplies they required expected never arrived. They needed to fight before they ran out. In a massive sea engagement, Octavian's fleet demolished the combined forces of Antony and Cleopatra, who both fled back to Egypt.

In 30, Octavian invaded. Both Antony and Cleopatra committed suicide. Octavian returned to Rome as a hero, and the Senate recognized his leadership, voting him a new title: Augustus. The word *imperator* was added after his name. It was the traditional title that victorious legions would give to their general. Its meaning in the Republic was something like "commander." But from Augustus forward the direct cognate is more appropriate. Emperor. Over the following decades, Augustus reformed the Roman state into the form of the Roman Empire we call the Principate (Wegen, 2012).

The Principate and the Role of Augustus

Augustus was 19 years old when Caesar was assassinated, and he was immediately thrust into a military and political role. He needed to be capable of dealing with two experienced and powerful opponents (Antony and Lepidus) and of manipulating the senators to act in his favor. He proved equal to the task. In hindsight, the rise and reign of Augustus may be the greatest example of political genius in history, certainly in the West.

He had been formally adopted by Caesar only six months before the assassination. Before the Ides of March, nobody was concerned about him. When Caesar died and his executioners fled, he wasn't considered a threat, and instead, Cicero and the other senators focused on Antony and his ambitions. Two months after March 15, 44 B.C.E., Octavian appeared on the Roman political scene to claim his place as Caesar's heir.

His first victory against Marc Antony was when he imposed on the Senate his decision to go to war against Caesar's executioners. Antony was an advocate for amnesty. Then, he was wily enough to frame his initiatives as a rebuilding of traditional Roman institutions. He played the patriotism card better than anyone; and, as Caesar's heir, he inherited tremendous wealth and the loyalty of many thousands of Caesar's veterans.

Once he put public opinion and the senators on his side to build legitimacy, he used the re-energized republican apparatus to strike. At first, Antony was the successor. After the Battle of Actium, the Senate welcomed Octavian as the hero who saved Rome.

The Principate

Octavian started using the title appointed by the Senate: Augustus, and in 27 B.C.E., he was named princeps, "first citizen." He was *primus inter pares*, "first among equals." The principate finds legitimacy in the *consensus universorum,* the agreement of all. It represents a collaboration between the Republic and the *princeps*. This collaboration is achieved by the power of the Senate to represent the will of the people (Kinder & Hilgemann, 1996).

Augustus rarely used the title of *imperator*, emperor, during his reign because he sought to avoid connotations of military enforcement of his regime. He veiled his power and made a show of restoring the forms of the Republic. Thus, between 27 and 23 B.C.E., he obtained the consulate and had the power of *imperium* over the territories under Roman influence. This meant he had ultimate *auctoritas* - executive power - supreme command over the army, the power to lead foreign policy, and control of the army.

In 23 B.C.E., he took on the *tribunicia potestas*, the power of a plebeian tribune, most importantly, the power to veto any governmental procedure. During the following two years, he continued to concentrate power and functions in his hands over almost every aspect of the political and economic life of Rome. In 19 B.C.E., he was granted *imperium* for life, and later, he was also appointed *Pontifex Maximus*, chief priest of Rome (Kinder & Hilgemann, 1996). Then, he also obtained the title of *pater patriae*, the father of his country, in 2 B.C.E.

While he concentrated all the political power, he was wise and astute enough to keep part of the republican structure: "The traditional magistracies that distributed power and state responsibilities were maintained, as were elections. Theoretically, nothing changed, except that they became essentially an ineffective formality, and Augustus assumed for himself a number of these powers for life" (Fernandes, 2022, para. 7).

Rome was a vast empire, and it needed more and better management, which was centered on the *princeps.* Augustus maintained the Senate, the bastion of the higher classes. However, he changed some of its traditional functions. To ensure his control over the Senate, he reduced it from 900 to 600 members and declared himself *princeps senatus,* "first man of the Senate." It continued to debate and pass laws, but he had the last say.

Augustus divided the provinces of the Empire into two groups: Senatorial and Imperial. The former were thoroughly Romanized and peaceful provinces, unlikely to rebel or be invaded by external threats. The Senate maintained the right to govern senatorial provinces just as it had governed them under the Republic – with proconsuls and propraetors. Imperial provinces, on the other hand, were on the frontiers and required large armies for defense or expansion. Augustus personally appointed legates as governors, usually experienced commanders. The system gave Augustus control of most of the army, but the Senate controlled the wealthiest and most stable territories.

Last but not least, the Senate lost the power to choose the consuls. Augustus would designate his successor. Regardless of the institutions that were preserved, the power became inherited, and therefore, the Republic didn't exist any longer.

Other Reforms

Once the political realm was stabilized and his power was ensured, Augustus launched a series of additional reforms. First, he had to take certain measures to improve the defense, government, and administration of a vast territory. Therefore, he introduced a series of military changes:

- He created a permanent standing army and raised the number of legions to 28.
- The fixed term of service for soldiers was set at 16 years and later increased to 20 years.
- He created a fund under his control to pay the soldiers' salaries, taking that power from the Senate and avoiding the misguided loyalty allowed by Marius' reforms.
- All those who enrolled as soldiers were considered Roman citizens with full rights and gained exemption from certain taxes.

Augustus' reforms helped separate the military from politics. The importance of the legions for the long-term stability of the Empire is part of the following chapter. Suffice it to say here that the Empire needed soldiers who would be loyal only to Rome and were eager to give their lives for it. Augustus' military changes ensured this.

In addition to military reform, Augustus installed a series of social initiatives to promote traditional Roman values:

- He promoted marriage by taxing single people and giving tax breaks for families with more children. He also criminalized adultery.

- He repaired old temples and dedicated new ones. As Pontifex Maximus, he revived many ancient rituals and sacrifices to present himself as a religious and moral leader.
- He sponsored a massive building and beautification program for Rome and other cities throughout the Empire.
- He reformed education and became a great patron of the arts, ushering in the Golden Age of Latin literature.
- Instituted social welfare for the urban poor and promoted games and festivals to foster Roman identity.

Augustus encouraged religious festivities and the worship of traditional Roman deities. However, he simultaneously created the imperial cult. Even though he declined the Senate's attempt to declare him a living god, Caesar was proclaimed Divus Iulius – "the Divine Julius." Augustus often included *Divi Filius* - "the son of God" – on official coinage and proclamations. However, the imperial cult was encouraged but not imposed, and at first the Roman citizens were reluctant to adopt such a deep transformation of their cherished traditions.

The Savior of Rome

Augustus was capable of creating a new political unit, pacified and stabilized, from the ruins of a Republic after a century of civil strife. His greatest accomplishment, however, wasn't to become an emperor without any significant opposition either from the people or from the traditional ruling elites. He was capable of persuading people that he was the best solution to save Rome from chaos. He ruled every aspect of the citizenry, and they didn't complain; on the contrary, the ruler became someone they could feel personally linked to. Augustus developed a new concept of political and popular leadership.

He dedicated himself to building an empire and also to his public image as the emperor the people needed. The greatest proof of his achievement is the *Res Gestae*, the inscription he spread across the territory of the *Imperium Romanum* celebrating his accomplishments: "he subjected the whole wide Earth to the rule of the Roman people" (Fernandes, 2022, para. 23). The text was completed after the emperor's death and carved on the walls of the Mausoleum of Augustus.

Essential Highlights

Even though the Ides of March were a turning point in the final dissolution of the Roman Republic, the old order's death warrant was signed as early as the murders of the Gracchi. Amid the chaos, a man paved his way to power, fighting against other men's ambitions and the reactionary power of the corrupted institutions of the moribund Republic. He was Augustus, the first Emperor of Rome.

He laid the foundations of a new era in Rome and created from out of nowhere a completely innovative conception of politics. The Republic as a political regime ended, but he created a new *res publica* to take its place.

As Augustus meticulously laid the Empire's cornerstones, he heralded not just a new era of governance but a Golden Age of peace and prosperity – the *Pax Romana*.

Chapter 8: The Pax Romana and the Height of the Empire

Give therefore your love and respect to the cause of peace, and to that capital in which we, conquerors and conquered, claim an equal right. –Tacitus

Two centuries, and not a single major conflict within Rome's borders. The *Pax Romana* – Roman Peace - wasn't just an era; it was Rome's magnum opus. It represents the age when Rome was the heartbeat of the known world.

This was a period of outstanding achievements in every realm: The Empire ensured the boundaries of its territory, and internal peace allowed unprecedented economic growth. Most of what is depicted about Rome in pop culture, and therefore, what is commonly known, comes from this period of high culture. Monumental buildings like the Roman amphitheaters and forums blend public spectacle with a political purpose to strengthen loyalty to Rome - and to the embodiment of Roman identity: The Emperor.

The *Pax Romana* also supported the emergence of the greatest names in Roman literature and philosophy. Arts and science flourish when society has solved its essential needs and can dedicate time and resources to the abstractions of human existence.

The Empire at Its Height

The *Pax Romana* is a period that covers the foundation of the Roman imperial system under Augustus Caesar in 27 B.C.E. to around 180 C.E., when Emperor Marcus Aurelius died (Campbell, 2022).

For a period of slightly over 200 years, 16 emperors ruled Rome. After Augustus' death in 14 C.E., the Julio-Claudian dynasty followed him on the throne: Tiberius, Caligula, Claudius, and Nero. Then, the Julio-Claudian family was replaced in 69 C.E., in a brief, one-year period of instability – The Year of the Four Emperors: Galba, Otho, Vitellius, and Vespasian. Vespasian was the first of the Flavian Emperors, and was followed by Titus and Domitian

(Beauchamp, n.d.). Then, the Five Good Emperors abandoned a dynasty based on bloodline. Rather, they chose successors through adoption (Encyclopedia Britannica, 2023). The Five Good Emperors were Nerva, Trajan, Hadrian, Antoninus Pius, and Marcus Aurelius (Beauchamp, n.d.).

The emperors of the *Pax Romana* continued to expand the boundaries of the *Imperium Romanum*, which reached its largest geographic area in 117 under Trajan. After his death, part of the conquered lands in Mesopotamia were soon lost, while the remaining frontiers were stable for the rest of the period.

At its peak, the territory of the Empire reached 2.75 million square miles (Zhou, 2015). It spanned from England, Portugal, and Morocco in the West to the Persian Gulf, Caspian Sea, and western Iran in the East (Vulic, 2023). Nearly 30 countries occupy that territory today.

The challenge wasn't limited to defending the boundaries from external enemies. It was a multiethnic empire with different languages, customs, and religious beliefs that needed to be either integrated or subjugated by the Romans to ensure peace and stability.

Pax Romana

The *Pax Romana* was much more than a period in the Empire's history: "It was above all an ideal. A cultural notion that fundamentally shaped the

Roman Empire and even our modern conception of what ordered living is" (Campbell, 2022, para. 3).

The *Pax Romana* didn't just happen; instead, it was the result of a series of policies intelligently implemented by Augustus. There were three potential flashpoints where Augustus needed to ensure peace. He had to enforce the borders and stability of an extensive and heterogeneous territory. He also needed to defend the Empire from foreign threats and prevent local rebellions. Finally, he had to be wary of the emergence of individual powers among the representatives of Rome within the confines of the state.

In Rome, Augustus had to consolidate his authority and control the traditional ruling class. Simultaneously, he had to create new sources of legitimacy for the government to appease social unrest. Historians have highlighted how Augustus was capable of taming the ambitions of the traditional ruling class while concentrating all power in the figure of the *princeps* - not as an autocrat but as the embodiment of the Roman *Res Publica*.

The *cursus honorum* survived, but only in name. Augustus created a new type of ruler, which was described by Tacitus in these terms: "Rome is not like primitive countries with their kings. Here, we have no ruling caste dominating a nation of slaves. You [the emperor] are called to be the leader of men who can tolerate neither total slavery nor total liberty" (Campbell, 2022, para. 18).

It's true Augustus continued the violent history of the last period of the Republic. He killed many of his rivals and eventually succeeded in putting the civil war to an end through a bloody victory. But once in power, he ensured the continuity of the Roman system. The *Pax Romana* was officially celebrated with the building of the *Ara Pacis Augustae* – the Altar of Augustan Peace.

Besides, the emperor pursued creating a "Roman style of life" imposed across the territory, from Hispania and West Africa to the Near East. Augustus and his successors installed a "civilizing" agenda over all the conquered people. While this was a direct benefit for Rome, it also brought prosperity and peace to the provinces and the inhabitants of the Empire. This view is open to criticism as being Romanocentric or Eurocentric. Indeed, the subject peoples of the Empire, particularly in the East and Africa had a long history of advanced culture – some longer than the Romans. Nevertheless, the standard of living under the Empire was higher for its subjects than for those who lived outside the *Imperium Romanum*.

Administrative Reforms

The previous chapter described many of the reforms Augustus carried out to transform Rome into a new political order that coalesced around the figure of the *princeps*. It wasn't a reformation of the state, but the creation of a new conception of politics where the individual power of the ruler isn't dissociated from the common interest.

Augustus implemented security measures in Rome and Italy. He instituted *vigiles,* or "watchmen," and urban legionary cohorts to patrol the streets with commanders under his direct orders. This extended the police power to around one per 100 inhabitants - far higher than in modern cities (Fuhrmann, 2011). This policy was extended to Italy, where he ordered the installation of military posts to discourage banditry and social upheavals. He also employed praetorian cohorts as personal bodyguards under his command, not that of the Senate.

However, he didn't always use direct intervention in the provinces, even those he was responsible for governing. This preserved a sense of autonomy. Instead, Augustus acted through intermediaries who eventually depended on him to remain in their positions and were thus compelled to obey his orders.

Besides increasing police presence in the provinces and the city, Augustus developed a system of post offices to enhance and accelerate communication within the Empire. It was called the *cursus publicus* and it transported official messages and tax revenues from one province to another. It used single messengers equipped with fast horses and light carriages called *rhedae.* The land speed average of the imperial courier service was about 50 miles per day (*The Cursus Publicus,* n.d.).

The Legions

The army always played a key role in the Roman society. It was closely connected with citizenship; it was a source of political participation in the form of the *comitia centuriata* that dated back to the Monarchy. It was a reflection of the hierarchical organization of society according to status. During the Republic, it had become a dangerous resource for growing individual power and hampering the state's stability.

However, during the *Pax Romana*, the period of expansion that started with the Republic continued until reaching its highest point with Trajan. And the larger and more heterogeneous the territory of the state was, the bigger the challenges faced by the emperors to preserve the Empire's cohesion. The Legions became the backbone of Roman identity in the Empire, especially for provincials. The legionaries represented the pinnacle of military power in the ancient world and the cornerstone of the Empire's stability and security.

The Roman legions evolved throughout Roman history. At all periods, they developed discipline, commitment, and loyalty. The loyalty might not have always been directed at the state, but it was loyalty nonetheless. A legion was formed of around 4,500 men, and then the number was raised to 5,200 and 6,000 at the peak of the Empire. This was paper strength, and when the Empire entered a deep crisis, attrition could lower the force of a legion to 1,000.

The legion was divided into 10 cohorts of 480 men, each organized into six centuries, each in turn led by a centurion.

Each century was divided into a *contubernium*: a group of eight soldiers who shared the same tent and responsibilities. Then they fought together, side by side, on the battlefield. This routine lasted for the entire 16, 20, or 24-year term of service for a legionnaire, depending on the current requirements (Bileta, 2023). It was an effective way to create strong bonds among the soldiers. Rome might have been too far away for them, or they could have felt their loyalty to their emperor faint, but on the battlefield, they fought to protect the band of brothers they belonged to.

Despite the discipline and superb strategies deployed by the Roman army, the legions weren't unbeatable: "The legion also suffered horrendous defeats. The most notable ones are the catastrophes at Cannae in 216 BC, Carrhae in 53 BC, and the Teutoburg Forest in 9 AD. In the latter, three legions were annihilated, never to be restored" (Bileta, 2023, para. 3).

The legions were feared and respected because they knew how to fight on the battlefield. The main goal for every soldier was to survive, and the best way to do it was through discipline. The general strategy of a legion in battle was to avoid casualties instead of killing more enemies. Victory was achieved by the capability of maintaining the battle line until the enemy was compelled to surrender (Zhou, 2015).

Roman equipment was well-suited to the task. It generally included a large semi-cylindrical shield called a *scutum*, a well-made helmet of bronze or iron, and metal armor, also of bronze or iron. The most common armor through the Republic and Empire was chain mail, *lorica hamata*, probably copied from the Gauls in the early 3rd century B.C.E. The most iconic Roman armor throughout the *Pax Romana* was the distinctive cuirass of segmented metal bands that we call *lorica segmentata*. It was incredibly durable and could defend against almost any weapon commonly in use at the time. But it was heavy.

Offensively, imperial Roman soldiers usually carried a heavy throwing spear called a *pilum*. A *pilum* was generally longer and heavier than most ancient javelins, but could also be used as a proper spear to ward off cavalry. Republican soldiers had carried two of slightly different sizes. The main weapon of the Roman legionary was his short sword, usually called a *gladius*. There were several different styles, but the *gladius* was mostly around 18 inches long, slightly waisted, and with a tapered point. While it was likely a thrusting weapon, the entire length of the blade was sharp on both sides. The Romans adopted the *gladius*, as they adopted most of their equipment, from their enemies. Early Roman historians use the term *gladius Hispaniensis* – the Spanish Sword.

Another core element of the legions' strategy was the multi-line formation and the organization of the soldiers into different cohorts that didn't attack at the same time. This avoided exposing all the troops to danger at the same time. It allowed Roman armies a tactical reserve, meaning they could bring in fresh reinforcements when needed during a battle.

The vast Roman Empire wasn't static, and the key to keeping it safe was to have a versatile and flexible strategy. Between Augustus' institution of the *principate* in 27 B.C.E. and Marcus Aurelius' death in 180 C.E., emperors developed different management styles of the legions and balanced expansionist military expeditions with the use of defensive forces to keep internal peace.

The Legions demanded the mobilization of the population and the expenditure of resources, which translated to a tax burden on the citizens. Therefore, emperors had to set priorities. Some emperors led more aggressive and expansionist strategies, moving the legions from one province to another wherever they were needed.

This entailed the risk of leaving a province unprotected in case of internal social unrest. Therefore, other emperors prioritized stability and left permanent garrisons in every province to ensure peace and keep the population under control (Zhou, 2015). Augustus had moved the legions out of Rome and placed them on the frontiers to reduce the risk of a plot against him. He used the Praetorian Guard instead to ensure his security. Nonetheless, in the future, the Praetorians became a mechanism to remove and install new emperors.

Economic Prosperity and the Role of Infrastructure

During the almost 200 years of the *Pax Romana*, the Empire reached unprecedented prosperity. The territory reached the peak of its expansion, and that meant an increase in arable land. Production rose and diversified, which was a boost for trading. On the other hand, the population of about 70 million people (*The Pax Romana*, n.d.) led to a higher demand for goods and a larger workforce to increase and accelerate production.

The Empire was divided into three economic regions. Europe included the lands of Great Britain, Italy, the Gauls (present-day France), the western region of Germany, and the Alps. The second region encompassed the provinces of Hispania (present-day Spain and Portugal) and northern Africa. The third region covered Greece, Egypt, and Asia Minor, including Palestine and Mesopotamia (Kinder & Hilgemann, 1996).

Besides keeping peace within and beyond the borders, the state played a key role in economic expansion. The increase in trading was enabled not only by the expanded demand and availability of diverse goods but also by the infrastructure. Augustus and the other emperors made significant investments to develop a network of roads and paved ways to connect all the corners of the Empire, and they all led to Rome. These roads and paths were used to transport goods for trading and to facilitate the movement of the army.

Even though the land routes were important, the state also promoted the use of sea transportation. To encourage this, the Romans built lighthouses and harbors in the main coastal cities. Since many goods were regional, the development of trading routes across the sea facilitated interregional trading. For instance, the oil produced in Egypt was taken to the south of Hispania. Furthermore, trading across the Mediterranean and the Black Sea intensified with regions outside the Empire, such as India, China, and southeastern Asia (Cartwright, 2018).

In addition to these public works, the Romans carried out monumental engineering works. They built bridges to connect the roads, aqueducts to provide cities and farms with water, and walls to protect the population from foreign invaders. The best example is Hadrian's Wall, built in 122 C.E. in the province of Britannia. The wall was finished in six years and crosses the island from side to side. It was built to prevent an invasion of the Picts from modern Scotland (Montoya, 2022).

Even though the large population demanded a lot of goods, it didn't imply the development of industrial production. Indeed, the landowners increased their incomes by selling their crops, including luxury goods (such as olives and wine), but there wasn't a massive interest among the aristocrats in investing in industry or commercial development. Instead, they wasted their fortunes on trivial expenditures. In the long term, the economy stagnated (Malvasi, 2023).

As in earlier periods, the wealth was concentrated in a few hands, and the number of poor and unemployed increased, in part due to the lack of jobs and the use of slave labor on plantations. To ensure food and avoid social turmoil, the state kept the price of grains artificially low and often distributed part of the harvest for free. While this avoided starvation for large parts of the population, it discouraged farmers and landlords from improving production as it didn't result in larger incomes (Malvasi, 2023).

Achievements of the Principate

Monumental Buildings

The economic splendor of the early Empire led to higher tax revenue, and this was used by the emperors to construct monumental buildings that didn't have a direct economic purpose but impacted the Romans' lives. When societies reach a high level of stability and economic development, citizens and the state can dedicate resources to leisure and non-productive activities.

During the *Pax Romana*, the Romans built public baths and amphitheaters in many important cities to provide the citizens with spaces to entertain themselves. Besides being a symbol of the Empire's greatness, these places were also used to enhance people's loyalty to their *princeps* and cultivate Roman identity.

Amphitheaters became a symbol of the Roman Empire's glory. These arenas could host thousands of spectators who attended to see the performances of gladiators. They reenacted epic battles from Rome's storied history and hosted public executions. They had fights between gladiators and soldiers, among gladiators, or against exotic beasts. Later, during the Christian persecutions, the spectacle consisted of beasts hunting and killing Christians who refused to renounce their faith and worship Roman deities.

Among the most famous amphitheaters, we can name the theater in Aspendos, built under Marcus Aurelius' reign; the Theatre of Orange, built by Augustus in present-day France; the Arena of Nîmes, built during the 1st century; and the most renowned, the Colosseum (Montoya, 2022).

The Colosseum, or *Amphitheatrum Flavium*, was started under Vespasian's reign, around 70–72 C.E., but was inaugurated by Titus in 80. He organized 100 days of games and public spectacles to celebrate (Montoya, 2022). It was a masterpiece of Roman architecture and engineering. It could host 50,000 spectators who could attend the shows protected from the sunlight by a retractable shade called a *velarium* (Encyclopedia Britannica, 2023). It also had underground tunnels with gates that led to the arena, where gladiators and animals waited for their turn to fight.

Cultural and Artistic Advances

During the *Pax Romana*, arts and culture flourished, also promoted by the state as a way to enhance Roman identity. It is the period of the blossoming of Roman literature and history. Augustus didn't want to be considered a despot king, so he invested time and resources to develop popular support based on a common national history.

Augustus asked Virgil to write a poem to create an image of him as the father of the nation and the protector of the people. Virgil wrote the *Eclogues, Georgics,* and *Aeneid* in Latin, the Empire's official language. These poems became an integral part of Western literature. The *Aeneid* tells the mythical story of how the Romans were linked to the people of

Troy and glorified the figure of the emperor (*Roman Culture and the Aeneid*, n.d.). Augustus learned early on how to use cultural production as a means of political propaganda.

The Golden Age of Latin literature also witnessed the emergence of other influential poets: Horace and Ovid. Horace lived when the Empire was being born. He was linked with Augustus and dedicated parts of his most famous poem, The Odes, to him. He also wrote charming poems about daily life in Rome.

Ovid's work also contributed to the creation of the Latin identity in the times of Augustus. He wrote the *Fasti*, an account of religious festivals recounting the early origins of Rome. In the poem, Ovid describes the royal family in a flattering way and with a great deal of patriotism. His greatest work was *The Metamorphoses*, a collection of stories from the creation of the universe to the death of Julius Caesar whose assassination and Civil War represent chaos. The Augustan Peace was the symbolic metamorphosis (Kenney, 2023).

Livy wrote the first official history of Rome. He wasn't the first historian to attempt to write the complete history of the nation, but unlike others, he didn't have a personal political interest. Instead, he had a moral approach to history. This was aligned with Augustus' project of installing moral ideas in imperial society (Ogilvie, 2023). Tacitus lived in the mature period of the Empire, during the rule of the Five Good Emperors. He contributed to building Roman history with a unique writing style and a sharp analysis of characters and events (McDonald, 20239).

The Golden Age of Rome also encompassed artistic achievements. Inspired and influenced by Greek artists, the Romans pursued all forms of artistic expression. Artistic production had many different purposes for the Romans: "Seal-cutting, jewelry, glassware, mosaics, pottery, frescoes, statues, monumental architecture, and even epigraphy and coins were all used to beautify the Roman world as well as convey meaning from military prowess to fashions in aesthetics" (Cartwright, 2017, para. 3).

The Romans created fascinating sculptures using different materials, including bronze and marble, for the most sophisticated pieces. The sculptures were characterized by detail and excessive realism. During the times of the *Pax Romana*, sculptures became bigger and dedicated to gods and emperors as a way to keep them alive forever.

Wall paintings and frescos were another distinguished form of art developed by the Romans. They used stucco to create real-life effects on the paintings in public buildings, private houses, temples, and walls all across the empire. One of the most famous is the House of Livia on the Palatine Hill, painted in the 1st century. It represents a 360° depiction of a garden. Another significant fresco was painted in the House of the Vettii in Pompeii before the eruption of Vesuvius in 79 C.E., which destroyed the city. These paintings reveal how the ancient

Romans lived and many of their values and beliefs (Becker, 2015).

Roman Stoicism

A philosophical school from Greece flourished in the Empire during the *Pax Romana*, and the last emperor of the period was one of the most important figures of the movement. The school of thought was called Stoicism and was founded by Zeno of Citium. The main idea was that our "ability to reason or consider action and consequence set humans apart from animals, and it could ultimately lead us to a better and more worthwhile existence. He (Zeno) also emphasized the importance of living in harmony with nature" (Lesso, 2022, para. 3).

In Rome, Stoicism had early philosophers who had worked with Cicero, although he wasn't a stoic himself. Later, this philosophical school gained importance with figures like Lucius Annaeus Seneca, a statesman under Nero; Epictetus, a slave of one of Nero's freedmen; and Marcus Aurelius, the famous emperor. Stoicism was characterized as a philosophy of life suitable for people of every station. It taught individuals to deal with the vicissitudes of life by developing endurance and strength and always acting consciously. Stoics believed there was a natural order to the universe, and individuals should learn to accept and follow the natural flow of events (Saunders, 2023).

The philosophy, widespread in Rome, was important for many political leaders who found key guidelines for ethical behavior in the Stoic principles. Nonetheless, the influence of Stoicism reached further than the political elite, and it was adopted by common people in daily life (*Did Stoicism Have Any Influence on Ancient Rome?* n.d.).

Essential Highlights

Augustus set the scene for the brightest period of Roman history: The largest expansion of the territory, the period of lasting peace, the safest moment for the Empire's boundaries, the greatest economic stability, and the flourishing of Roman culture. The first emperor started the reforms, and the following rulers continued to develop and ensure the Empire's success.

While the sun shone brightly on Rome during the *Pax Romana*, no empire is immune to decay. The 3rd century brought crisis to Rome, and the challenges of a fading Golden Age.

Chapter 9: The Crisis of the Third Century and the Late Empire

How does a mighty empire like Rome, at the pinnacle of its glory, find itself spiraling into chaos in just a matter of decades?

During the 3rd century C.E., the Roman Empire entered an era of decline and uncertainty. The focus inevitably sets on the many problems that hampered social, economic, and political stability, leading to a crisis that put the state in danger after over two centuries of peace. Nonetheless, this period also reveals the tenacity and resilience that undergirded the Empire and enabled it to adapt and reshape itself.

The crisis of the 3rd century represents a turning point in the Western Empire and the beginning of its end; at the same time, the Byzantine Empire rose in the East, and it would carry Rome's legacy for another millennium.

Internal and External Threats to Roman Power

The Barbarians

The Barbarians were several Germanic tribes that lived beyond the limits of the Empire's boundaries, didn't speak Latin, and were considered savage by the Romans. The term was indistinctly used by the Romans to refer to any foreign people who didn't fall under the Roman concept of civilization. The term included the German, Celtic, Hunnic, and Slavic peoples from the northeast, among many others (*Barbarian Origin, Invasions and Kingdoms*, 2023).

From the Roman perspective, the presence of barbarian tribes had hampered the *Imperium Romanum* since the time of the Republic. Julius Caesar had fought against them during his campaigns against the Gauls, and Augustus consolidated the northeastern frontier at the Rhine and Danube Rivers (Britannica Encyclopedia, 2023). During the centuries of imperial splendor, Rome fought against foreign tribes and succeeded in pushing them away from Roman lands.

In 200 C.E., Germanic tribes coming from the Scandinavian Peninsula started a slow but massive and persistent migration into Central Europe. The Goths, Vandals, Burgundians, and the Gepidae left their lands in the north and headed southeast toward the Black Sea. These German tribes weren't nomadic; they migrated to settle in new lands where they could be established permanently. They settled in present-day Germany and the lands between the Weser and Vistula rivers. Later, they reached the Danube and settled near the Roman frontier (Britannica Encyclopedia, 2023).

As the Germanic tribes approached the Empire's boundaries, they pushed the local tribes into Roman territory. This was the mass migration's first impact on the Roman population and became a factor in destabilizing the frontiers, which were very far away from the capital by then (Kinder & Hilgemann, 1996).

From 150 on, the Barbarians spread across the Roman periphery, causing unrest among the local populations. The Romans fought and repelled the

Marcomanni and the Alemanni in Italy under Marcus Aurelius. This was the first time a hostile force reached the peninsula since the German invasions repelled by Gaius Marius in 101 B.C.E. Nevertheless, the pressure continued, and many Germans established themselves inside the empire by 260 C.E. The Saxons and Franks violently ravaged the North and Britannia (Britannica Encyclopedia, 2023). By the middle of the 3rd century, the Goths and the Heruli pillaged the Black Sea and the Aegean.

The Goths entered and settled the Balkan Peninsula and Asia Minor and forced the Romans to abandon the northern Danube region. More tribes arrived: the Quadi, the Iazyges, the Sarmatians, and the Vandals, among others. Despite Roman attempts to defend their position, the army could not stem the tide of the invaders (Badian et al., 2023).

In the East, the Sassanid Persians replaced the Parthian empire, which had been weakening for centuries. By the middle of the 3rd century, the Romans had fought a long and exhausting campaign. Even though Emperor Aurelian reestablished unity through much of Roman territory in the 270s, the Empire lost all of its remaining land in Mesopotamia (Badian et al., 2023).

The external threat was an unbeatable problem for the Roman Empire due to its lack of satellite states to buffer the advance of enemy forces. This eventually led to the abandonment of the peripheral provinces or the foundation of foreign kingdoms (Kinder & Hilgemann, 1996). The legions' defeat in their attempt to repel the invasions proved the weakness of a widely extensive frontier that Rome couldn't defend properly.

Rome lost territories at the hands of the invaders and had to accept foreign tribes within its borders, which brought new issues threatening governability and weakened the central political apparatus in Rome.

Military Anarchy

The assassination of Emperor Alexander Severus in 235 C.E. triggered a crisis in political power and a shift in the Roman leadership paradigm. During this period, the Empire required more troops to control social unrest and repel external threats. This was a time of warrior emperors who were backed up by their troops. But in consequence, it was also a period of deep instability - any general who had military power could seize the throne.

The emperors raised by military means are called the "Barracks Emperors." Many emperors were installed by the army and remained on the throne for as long as they could retain the support of their troops (Mark, 2017). The empire had 24 emperors in less than 100 years. Before that, 26 emperors had ruled for 250 years (Bileta, 2023).

It was a time of anarchy because the rulers depended on violence to hold the throne. The unity of the Empire was torn, and it split into three parts, taking it close to collapse. In 260 C.E., the provinces of Gaul, Hispania, and Britain broke away to form the Gallic Empire. In the east, by 267, Egypt, Palestine, and Syria had also formed the independent Palmyrene Empire.

The Economic and Social Crisis

The Barbarian invasions coincided with a series of social and economic changes that led to new political struggles. On one hand, the regions neighboring the Empire in Asia and Africa developed an advanced agricultural system. It posed fierce competition for Roman production (Kinder & Hilgemann, 1996).

The *villae*, or country estates, of Rome's elite, became important political and cultural centers, and the differences between the cities and the rural areas deepened. The upper class of landlords became wealthier and monopolized political power, with growing influence in their lands far from the capital (Kinder & Hilgemann, 1996).

On the other hand, slavery withdrew due to the halt in territorial expansion. This impacted the workforce, which was then replaced by an increasing group of free peasants or *coloni* (*Crises of the Roman Empire*, n.d.). They settled on their own lands and worked for themselves, but were compelled to pay high taxes to the local authorities. Their properties and crops were constantly looted by the Barbarians. This group slowly resigned their rights as property owners to the elites in return for protection. This represents the first seeds of a system that would develop into Medieval peasant serfdom.

The production switched focus to subsistence goods, which caused a decline in trading, accompanied by the violent situation in several regions. Local economies became self-sufficient, and people moved from the cities to the countryside looking for the means to survive. It meant the decline of urban life and a decrease in cross-Empire trade (*Crises of the Roman Empire*, n.d.).

The Dominate: Diocletian and Constantine

The first emperor to introduce reforms to avoid the Empire's collapse was Aurelian (270–275). He reunified the Empire by defeating the emperors of the independent but short-lived Gallic and Palmyrene Empires. Then, he increased the security at the borders to reduce the impact of Barbarian pressure. Finally, he elevated the position of the emperor above the people and the military generals to reduce their power. However, there were many structural issues that needed further reform.

Diocletian's Tetrarchy

Diocletian ruled between 284 and 305 and is credited with putting the 3rd-century crisis to an end. He reorganized the administration and government of the Empire by establishing a "tetrarchy," or "rule of four," and settled the new administrative and political centers in Nicomedia (modern Turkey), Mediolanum (Milan), Sirmium (in modern Serbia), and Trier, Germany. These cities were closer to the borders of the Empire and needed closer oversight and stronger defense (Diocletian and the Tetrarchy, n.d.). Each of these four areas was further subdivided into *dioceses*, 12 in total.

The tetrarchy had two senior emperors, called *augusti,* and two junior emperors, called *caesares.* The *augusti* ruled from Mediolanum and Nicomedia, while the *caesares* administered Trier and Sirmium. Since each region was autonomous and self-sufficient, it led to conflicts between the four states (Woolf, 2012).

Diocletian continued Aurelian's trend of building the emperor's authority, fueling his imperial persona with ceremonies and building projects. This change in the fundamental role of the emperor in Roman society represents the end of the Principate founded by Augustus. This later period became known to scholars as the Dominate. Diocletian promoted more military campaigns to control the frontiers and social unrest. All this increased the state's expenditures and led to taxation reform (*Diocletian and the Tetrarchy,* n.d.).

Constantine and the New Capital

The tetrarchy became a source of confusion. But in 306 C.E. Constantine I was pronounced *augustus* by his troops at Eboracum (modern York) in Britannia. He consolidated his power through civil war in the West, defeating his rival Maxentius in 312 at the Battle of the Milvian Bridge just outside Rome.

Legends surround the battle. Constantine's mother, Helena, was a Christian from Asia Minor. It is impossible to determine Constantine's thoughts about his mother's religion at the time of the battle, but tradition holds that he witnessed a radiant cross in the sky shortly before his forces met those of Maxentius, accompanied by the Greek words *en toutoi nika*. The Latin tradition has adopted the phrase *in hoc signo vinces* – "In this sign, you will conquer." Constantine adorned his troops' shields with a cross, and they carried the day, giving him control of the Western Empire.

In 313 C.E., Constantine enacted the Edict of Milan to establish religious tolerance within the Empire. During the past three centuries, Christianity had spread across the Roman world. Christians were persecuted because their beliefs clashed with Roman traditions. Constantine sought internal peace and new ways to bring cohesion to the collective Roman identity (*Constantine*, n.d.).

In 324, Constantine became sole emperor when he defeated Licinius I at the first Battle of Adrianople on the European side of the Bosporus. In an attempt to reinforce the empire's security and improve administration, he moved the capital to Byzantium (present-day Istanbul, Turkey). He changed the capital's name to Constantinople, bringing art and ornaments from Rome (History.com Editors, 2023).

Constantine expanded the administrative apparatus to 14 *dioceses*, built a wall to protect Constantinople, and provided lands to noblemen to ensure his position. To populate the city, he offered free food rations to new residents and built infrastructure, such as aqueducts, to improve the quality of life. Constantine made the new capital the heart of the Empire, framed by Roman law and Christian beliefs, but adopted the Greek language in contrast to Latin. This reinforced the cultural division between the Western and Eastern Empires.

In 337, Constantine died. He had converted to Christianity and was baptized at some point before his death. It's impossible to determine the exact date of his conversion, as there are varying traditions. Nevertheless, he made important contributions to spreading Christianity throughout the Empire (Encyclopedia Britannica, 2023). His building program included the Church of the Holy Sepulchre in Jerusalem and the original Basilica of Saint Peter in Rome. In addition, he called the first Council of Nicaea in 215, which produced the original version of the Nicene Creed – a codified statement of belief meant to unite the diverse communities of Christians throughout the Roman Empire and beyond.

Constantine's dynasty would last for five generations until Julian the Apostate, the last pagan emperor, died in 363 C.E. Thereafter, the Valentinian and Theodosian Dynasties would rule from 364 to

457. However, there was a dizzying array of usurpers and intermarriages, and there were often several emperors ruling different parts of the Empire simultaneously. The final division of the old *Imperium Romanum* into the Western Empire and the Byzantine Empire came upon the death of Theodosius I in 395. His sons, Arcadius and Honorius, became rulers in the East and West, respectively (Phelan, 2022).

Essential Highlights

The 3rd century was marked by crisis and anarchy. The choice of emperor was often in the hands of the military, causing extreme instability and violence. This was fueled by the Barbarian invasions, which had started before but intensified. And the defenseless population living on the borders suffered from constant attacks and looting. Chaos was deepened by social unrest due to the economic crisis and a progressive loss of civil rights for peasants.

Emperors Diocletian and Constantine attempted to save the Empire by reinforcing the imperial authority, improving the administration, enhancing the frontiers' defense, and keeping the political system intact. They enjoyed relative success since they avoided the collapse, and the Western Empire endured for almost 150 years after Constantine's death. However, the old *Imperium Romanum* was horrendously decayed. As reforms and religious transformations brought temporary relief to a beleaguered Empire, the relentless march of time and fate continued.

Chapter 10: The Fall of the Western Roman Empire

Every empire has its sunset, and for the mighty Western Roman Empire, dusk approached with a series of events that shook the ancient world. After the invasion of Hannibal over 600 years before, no Roman ruler or citizen could ever imagine that the Eternal City would ever fall. However, the moment arrived, and the glorious Empire collapsed under its own weight.

The year 476 C.E. became a milestone in Western Civilization. That year, the Western Empire fell, and it meant the end of a monumental era. Moreover, it represented the end of Antiquity. The world, as it was known, would never be the same, with Rome as the epicenter of power and the lighthouse of culture. For almost a millennium, Rome set the pace for much of the progress of the West. After its collapse, everything had to be rebuilt.

Even though the Empire as a political unity collapsed in the West, it endured for another 1,000 years in the East, keeping the Roman flame alive and spreading its influence. Rome shaped subsequent civilizations and underscored lessons to glean from its rise and fall. Rome isn't a lost relic but the foundation stone of human progress.

Reasons for the Western Empire's Fall

Similar to the 3rd-century crisis, the fall of the Empire was the result of many factors. Many of them had their origins in the 3rd century or even earlier, and despite several emperors' attempts, the stress on the administrative, social, economic, and military infrastructure was too great. Political and economic instability deepened, and social unrest rose. The final blow was delivered by the Barbarians who had raided the Empire's borders since the 2nd century.

Political Instability

After Constantine established his capital at Byzantium, and renamed it Constantinople, Rome stopped being the center of political and economic power. The Eternal City quickly declined. Progressively, the eastern provinces became more powerful, and Constantinople surpassed Rome's influence. In the West, other cities such as Ravenna and Milan occupied the place of the old capital. The emperors moved out of Rome and hardly ever went to visit it, although it was still the largest and most populated city in Europe (*Roman Empire Politics,* n.d.).

Even though the decision to divide the Empire was made to improve border defense, streamline tax collection, and reduce local powers that could overshadow the emperor, it was only successful in the

East. The division of the state brought religious and linguistic barriers that became obstacles instead of fostering cooperation to hold the Empire (*Roman Empire Politics*, n.d.).

Diocletian had organized a tetrarchy to avoid plots against the emperors by appointing two co-rulers (one for the West and one for the East), the *augusti*. Each of them was supported by a *caesar*. It was supposed to avoid weakness by having a successor in place before an emperor died or abdicated. However, Diocletian's experiment failed in the early 4th century, leading to constant civil wars (Bileta, 2023).

After the crisis of the 3rd century, the sources of legitimacy that had once kept the vast Empire cohesive were discredited. The emperor, who was in the past the embodiment of the *res publica*, and the Senate, the remaining symbol of Rome's ancient noble pedigree, were infected with corruption. The long process of economic evolution had contributed to concentrating impressive fortunes in the hands of the few who had the power to buy votes and seize power. An emperor could be easily overthrown if the opposition had enough support.

This internal instability hampered the ability to control local powers, social turmoil, and the more frequent attacks launched by the Barbarians.

Economic Decline

The economic decline is linked to the Empire's territorial fragmentation and the halt of outward expansion. The late Empire didn't obtain new lands or slaves to reward the legions and increase production. The slavery system had created a large gap between the rich and the poor, and that difference sharpened when the wealthy landowners charged the *coloni* with higher taxation (*The Fall of Rome*, n.d.).

As production capacity declined, the Empire's expenses continued to increase. Public funds were allocated to building public works such as aqueducts, bridges, and roads, which were key to supporting the expansion and better administration of a vast state. Grand public works like baths, amphitheaters, and monuments, had a symbolic purpose and were key to maintaining political cohesion and a strong centralized power. However, the bulk of the budget was used to pay the army.

The Roman legions had been the backbone of the state since the times of the Republic. At first, they were the means to conquer new lands, but after the 3rd century C.E., the legions were used mostly to repel the Barbarian invaders. Therefore, Rome faced higher expenses but won nothing. On the contrary, they slowly lost many important territories.

In the past, the main connection between the generals and the legionaries who spent years fighting for Rome far away from their homes was loyalty and a sense of belonging. Over time, that loyalty loosened, and the state had to continuously increase soldiers' salaries to avoid a rebellion or desertion.

Emperors faced a double problem: increasing costs and less income. On one hand, they attempted to increase the tax revenue, but most of the tax collection was concentrated in the provinces. The generals and other officers in the distant provinces collected taxes and used them at their own discretion. From their perspective, they were at the outer confines of the Empire, dealing with the Barbarians. The bond with Rome as the core of the state was broken. This added to the increasing levels of corruption (Gill, 2019). Money from taxes didn't reach Rome.

On the other hand, emperors tried to increase their income by making more money. The denarius was a silver coin developed in the 3rd century B.C.E. and survived through the Empire. Under the early emperors, the *denarius* was made of 75% silver and 25% base. During the crisis of the 3rd century, the emperors reduced the amount of silver in the coins to double the production. This allowed them to manufacture more coins. But, far from solving the problem, it led to runaway inflation (Calvo & Quintana, 2022). The value of the currency fell, and prices rose, causing a sharp drop in trading, tax collection, and people's purchasing power.

As the external threats increased the tension, more military forces were needed, and this situation deepened. Meanwhile, internal cohesion and the common values that once held Roman society together had vanished.

Military Challenges

The importance of the legions for Rome in times of expansion and after the beginning of the Barbarian invasions has been explained. The civil wars triggered by the usurpers and emperors fighting for power had diverted the military to focus on internal issues. Meanwhile, the Barbarian attacks became more aggressive and frequent.

This chaotic situation witnessed a sharp decline in the Roman legions. In the past, becoming a soldier was considered a Roman citizen's right. After the 3rd century, it was harder to recruit legionaries. Campaigns were longer, they had to remain for more years in the military service, and the rewards weren't attractive. Therefore, the generals began to admit non-Roman citizens to join the troops.

Many of those non-Roman inhabitants of the provinces were Barbarian people who had settled in Roman territory and blended with the local population. The blending process took place over centuries. Some historians have called it the "barbarization of the army." "In states of warfare of the third century, Emperors and their rivalries picked up soldiers from these tribes that stayed within the borders of the empire and these soldiers were given the commands of Roman commanders as mercenaries" (Gazioğlu, n.d., p. 2).

In Italy, men were more interested in achieving administrative positions and the recruitment rate continued to decrease (Vulic, 2023). The desperate need for more soldiers led the Romans to admit mercenaries. First, they were hired soldiers who didn't fight for their nation but for money.

In the times of the tetrarchy, emperors made drastic changes. They gave lands to Frankish tribes in Gaul in exchange for military cooperation to fight against the Huns. Emperor Constantine used the Vandals to defend the province of Pannonia in the northern Balkans, leaving the Vandal generals to carry out the recruitment. After a catastrophic loss at the second Battle of Adrianople, Theodosius admitted the Goths into the Balkans as *foederati*, allies, and paid them in exchange for peace and military support. In the East, the emperors admitted Arabic troops led by their generals to help the Romans hold their borders (Gazioğlu, n.d.).

In the long term, this had deleterious consequences for the army. The foreign generals and soldiers could never be effectively "Romanized," and the new troops lacked allegiance to the Empire. On the contrary, the Barbarians imposed many of their own customs. In the 4th century, thousands of Germans enlisted in the army and imposed their terms and practices, such as the *be*, an old Germanic battle cry (Frye, 2007).

This tendency resulted in the fragmentation of morale and cohesion that had made the legions nearly invincible for centuries. Moreover, it undermined the traditional military aristocracy since service was neither a privilege nor a profitable business. Even though there were new laws against the Barbarians, such as forbidding marriage between ethnic groups, the Germans had become predominant in many regions of the Empire (Frye, 2007).

In sum, the Barbarians weren't only an external threat; they were behind the Roman lines and even became a predominant cultural element in much of Europe.

Social Fragmentation

The transformation within the army also coincided with a shift in the connection between common people and the army. While many admired the Barbarians for their strength and military power and approved of their incorporation into the army, most of the population feared them. They had witnessed the violent raids against the villages on the frontiers. The provincial citizens had suffered through the devastation of their lands and had lost everything to the hands of those who were then received as Roman citizens in a privileged position. For common people, barbarians in the Roman army were mercenaries.

Besides the challenges faced by the army and the significant wealth disparity, there was another factor causing social dislocation: religious diversity. As mentioned, the Edict of Milan ended the formal persecution of Christians within the Empire. However, it triggered a new cultural transformation that worked against Roman cohesion.

The law of religious tolerance and the increasing presence of Christianity undermined many ancient Roman traditions. Moreover, it became a political factor since Christians considered the god of Abraham the highest source of power and authority, above the emperor or homeland (*The Fall of the Roman Empire*, n.d.). It wasn't only a matter of individual faith but also a shift in the concept of citizenship. This contradiction between religious belief and citizenship at such a large scale was new within the Empire.

In the Eastern Empire, Christianity effectively served as a new moral background to hold political unity. However, it led the West into deeper fragmentation. The Church emerged as a parallel source of power. Historically, the chief priest of the Roman state was the Pontifex Maximus. Under the Empire, the emperors assumed the title. However, it is possible some Christian bishops of Rome may have used the title after the rule of Constantine. Even though Christianity blended with many Roman traditions, struggles emerged, adding to the conflicting relations with the pagan practices of Romans who refused to convert and the foreign Germanic tribes (*Did Christianity Cause the Fall of Rome?* n.d.).

The Scourge of God

The Barbarians, who had started a massive migration in the 3rd century, didn't stop moving across Europe. Wherever they reached, they caused problems by displacing the local population, attacking the communities and lands on the frontier, or settling inside the territory of the Roman Empire.

The Roman emperors employed many strategies to deal with the invaders. In the 4th century, German groups settled in the confines of the Empire, and to avoid war, the emperors allowed them to stay as *foederati,* allies. In exchange, Rome demanded their support to defend the frontier from other invaders that came from the Asian steppes.

In 376 C.E., a group coming from Central Asia challenged the integrity of the Empire. They were the Huns, a nomadic people who had settled in the Hungarian plains. They had been displaced from their original lands and approached the Roman frontiers searching for the resources they needed to build their own Empire. The Huns attacked other Barbarian tribes like the Goths and the Burgundians in present-day France.

But the Huns weren't the Romans' only problem. They were simultaneously fighting the Vandals in Hispania and northern Africa. The Empire didn't have the powerful legions to move from one part to another, so taking the troops out of Italy left the old capital unprotected.

From 434 to 453, the Huns were led by Attila. He was called "the Scourge of God" because of the cruelty and violence he displayed toward the populations living in the Empire. Many considered his attacks on both the Eastern and Western Empires to be divine punishment. In 451, a Roman-Visigothic alliance defeated Attila at the Battle of the Catalaunian Plains in Gaul.

However, in 452, Attila and the Huns took advantage of Rome's weak defenses and launched an invasion of Italy that would have ended in Rome's destruction (Jarus, 2022). Emperor Valentinian III sent a delegation to meet Attila that included Pope Leo I (*What really stopped Atilla the Hun?* 2007).

It is uncertain what happened in that meeting. Some scholars suggest the Pope used Attila's superstitions against him. Alaric the Goth had sacked the city in 410 C.E. but had died shortly afterward. Others believe that Rome was nothing but a pile of ruins and Attila searched for wealth in vain. Whatever happened between Attila and the Pope, the invasion stopped, and Attila turned his attention to the East. However, he could never accomplish his objective of attacking Byzantium because he died under mysterious circumstances on the night of his wedding in 453 (Jarus, 2022). The Hunnic coalition soon disintegrated.

Attila and the Huns didn't cause the Empire's collapse, but they exposed the fragility of its defenses. It was only a matter of time.

The Final Blow

By the time the Ostrogoths reached Rome in 476, the Empire was barely a shadow of its former self. Besides the Huns, the Vandals and the Visigoths had also ravaged Italy, contributing to Rome's destruction.

The Visigoths under Alaric sacked Rome in 410 C.E. shortly after the emperor Honorius had moved the Western capital to Ravenna. However, they besieged Ravenna and compelled the emperor to pay tribute in exchange for an armistice. The Visigoths continued their migration and settled around Toulouse, France, where they founded their kingdom on the border of Italy.

The Vandals had crossed Europe from east to west, pushed by the Visigoths. The Romans attempted to keep them beyond their borders for decades, but they eventually crossed the Rhine and settled in Gaul, admitted as *foederati* in 405 C.E. However, the Vandals were again pushed by the Visigoths and crossed the Pyrenees to settle in Hispania in 409. Shortly after, they crossed to Africa, still under Roman power, and founded a kingdom in modern Tunisia.

At first, the Romans allowed the Vandal kingdom and split control of the coastline with them. But in 439, the Vandals surprisingly sacked Carthage. The Vandals' expansion wasn't over, and the Romans tried to ensure peace. The attempt failed and the Vandals attacked Rome in 455. Just like when Attila had approached the gates of Rome three years before, Pope Leo I negotiated: The Vandals agreed not to kill the citizens, destroy buildings, or set the city on fire. In exchange, the gates of Rome were opened, and the invaders despoiled the Eternal City of treasures and carried off some of the citizens to slavery (Vulic, 2023).

Odoacer

During the 5th century, Rome was sacked on three occasions – first, by the Visigoths in 410, then by the Vandals in 455. In 476, Rome was ravaged again, but this time, the throne passed to a Barbarian king.

In 475, the Roman general Orestes was proclaimed *magister militum,* master of the army. Orestes wanted to control the throne, so he exiled emperor Julius Nepos and appointed his own young son, Romulus Augustulus, as the new emperor. Orestes lacked military support within Italy and the rest of the Western Empire; moreover, Constantinople refused to recognize Romulus as legitimate. Orestes only had his Barbarian *foederati* under Odoacer's command to rely on (*Odoacer and the Fall of Rome*, n.d.).

Scholars are unsure of Odoacer's origins, but he was likely Sciri (Mark, 2014). The Sciris (or Scirians) were a small Germanic tribe that had settled in present-day Poland and joined the Goths to fight the Huns. Eventually, they were absorbed by the

Ostrogoths, the tribe that moved into Italy as *foederati* and whom Odoacer now led (*Kingdoms of the Germanic Tribes*, n.d.).

In exchange for their support, the Barbarians demanded lands within Italy, but their request was denied because the area was already populated. Odoacer wasn't satisfied with Orestes' refusal to attend to their demands and raised his tribes against him. On August 23, 476, the Barbarians proclaimed Odoacer as their king and executed Orestes in Placentia (present-day Piacenza). Then they marched to Rome and deposed Romulus Augustulus, who was only a child. Odoacer seized power and named himself king, the first Barbarian king of Italy (Britannica Encyclopedia, 2023). The Western Empire was officially gone.

Essential Highlights

The Crisis of the 3rd Century dealt a death blow to the Roman Empire, but it took almost two more centuries to manifest its destructive effects. The emperors' attempts to save Rome were enough to hold the Eastern Empire, but the West couldn't resist the internal contradictions that undermined the traditional pillars of power. The thriving economy and a solid political authority no longer existed, and the army was more of a challenge to imperial integrity than the traditional backbone it had always been.

The Barbarians were already inside the Empire. The series of successive Barbarian attacks on Rome wasn't the illness but the symptom. Odoacer only landed the final strike at what were already the ruins of the Roman Empire.

While the sun set on the Western Roman Empire, the embers of its civilization still burned brightly, influencing ages to come. As we journey toward the conclusion, let's reflect on Rome's enduring legacy and the indelible mark it left on all of human history. The spirit of Rome beckons you to delve deeper, to explore its enigmas and marvels, and to keep its memory alive.

Conclusion

Rome has grown since its humble beginnings, and it is now overwhelmed by its own greatness. −Titus Livius

The history of the Western world started thousands of years ago, in prehistoric times when people first learned to cultivate crops, organize themselves to build their houses and cities, and dominate nature. Ancient Italy was one of the epicenters where civilization as we know it took its first steps. The ancient Italic tribes are proof of the constant and uninterrupted progress of humankind. They built a long-lasting and flourishing culture that not only transcended the peninsula but also set the pace for the whole ancient world.

Romulus and Remus' mythical story was a precursor to what Rome was meant to be. Saved by the god Mars, they were destined to lead the kingdom that would rule the known world and expand it. Like most mythical stories of greatness, it required a touch of tragedy. Romulus assassinating his brother to be the only king was the prelude to the troubled history of Rome. It was the first stage of an alternation of splendor and crisis. For the ancient Romans, each moment of weakness became the perfect challenge to showcase resilience and emerge stronger and wiser.

Throughout these pages, we have seen Rome become a powerful kingdom and set the basis for most contemporary forms of political organization. We have witnessed how people fought for their rights to make law and justice the framework of social life during the Republic. The Romans didn't stop when they overcame their struggles and neither the rulers nor the common people settled for less. They sought glory and built the path to achieve it. It is a powerful lesson that still resonates whenever the name of the Eternal City is recalled.

The many centuries of the Roman Empire are a metaphor for human nature: How far ambition and conviction can take us, and how destructive both can be as well. Romans transformed the world and fell victim to their own changes. Despite the controversies that entailed their dominance of people and lands, it is unquestionable that they shaped the modern world, from Great Britain to the distant lands surrounding the Indus River in Asia. They had a vision and a purpose, and they triumphed, even after their collapse.

Ancient Rome's enduring legacy reaches us today. They remain one of the greatest empires in history for several reasons. Firstly, they covered vast territories at their peak. Additionally, they governed millions of people under their laws, who were categorized as subjects or citizens, a distinction created by the Empire and still relevant in contemporary societies. They imposed a Roman worldview but also embraced and blended with other cultures.

Extensive and multicultural, the Roman civilization lasted for almost 1,000 years in the West, and the Eastern Empire survived for another 1,000. Still, their legacy remains alive: "Roman inventions or innovations were so effective that they either continued in use or were later rediscovered to serve as models in virtually every aspect of human society, from the mundane to the sublime" (Mark, 2020). If we look around, we have inherited from the ancient Romans architectural and artistic styles, institutions, laws, and rights, a universal religion, and a language that is the root of many contemporary languages.

As the curtains draw on the grand narrative of Rome, remember: its legacy is not just in ruins and ancient texts but in the DNA of all the civilizations that followed. Don't let this be the end of your journey into Rome's majestic past. Dive deeper, explore more, and let the spirit of the Romans inspire you to greater understanding and wisdom. Let the history of Rome be a beacon, guiding you to uncharted territories of knowledge. Forge ahead, for many more tales are waiting to be discovered, and Rome's echoes call out to you!

The ancient Romans brought their culture and worldview with them wherever they went. They left their trace in every corner of the world where they settled their population or stationed their legions. They carried the light of civilization and spread the message of a thriving culture. Part of what we are today, wherever you are reading this, keeps the essence of the ancient Romans. We are compelled to continue with their mission and keep alive their legacy. *Valete*! (Farewell!)

Note to the Reader

Sharing sincere feedback is the best way to support (and improve) the work of independent publishers. If you enjoyed and found value in this book, please leave a review and invite others to learn about and reflect upon our common past to build a promising future.

References

10000 years of economy - Failure of the Gracchi's reforms. (n.d.). Citeco.fr. https://www.citeco.fr/10000-years-history-economics/antiquity-to-middle-ages/failure-of-the-gracchi-s-reforms#:~:text=He%20proposed%20an%20agricultural%20reform,charged%20with%20enacting%20the%20law

6.5: The Seven Kings. (2020, August 8). Chemistry LibreTexts. https://chem.libretexts.org/Courses/Lumen_Learning/Book%3A_Western_Civilization_(Lumen)/Ch._05_Early_Roman_Civilization_and_the_Roman_Republic/06.5%3A_The_Seven_Kings

Adam, B. (2023, November 27). *The Vandals, an infamous Germanic tribe that sacked Rome.* The Roman Empire. https://roman-empire.net/people/vandals/

Ancient Roman monarchy - (753 BC – 509 BC). (n.d.). Rome.net. https://www.rome.net/roman-monarchy#:~:text=Romulus%2C%20son%20of%20the%20god,Rome%20a%20body%20of%20laws

Ancient Roman monarchy: Timeline and overview. (2015, January 15). Study.com. https://study.com/academy/lesson/ancient-roman-monarchy-timeline-lesson-quiz.html.

Ancient Rome. Romulus and Remus. (2015, March 16). History Learning Site. https://www.historylearningsite.co.uk/ancient-rome/romulus-and-remus/#google_vignette

Ancient Rome—Early Republic. (n.d.). Heritage History. https://www.heritage-history.com/index.php?c=resources&s=study-qdiv&h=ancient_rome&f=republic

Ancos. (2018, June 11). *Italy 01: During Prehistory.* Life in Italy. https://lifeinitaly.com/italy-prehistoric/

Augustan army reforms. (n.d.). https://faculty.washington.edu/alain/CLAS.HS TAM330/ArmyReforms.html

Badian, E., Salmon, E.T., Forsythe, G.E., Ferguson, J., Hornblower, S., Vermeule, E.D. Townsend, P.P., MacMullen, Ramsay, S., Richard P., & Grummond, N.T. (n.d.). Ancient Rome. In *Encyclopedia Britannica.* Retrieved December 13, 2023 from https://www.britannica.com/place/ancient-Rome. Accessed 3 January 2024.

Barbarian origin, invasions and kingdoms. (2023, May 23). Study.com. https://study.com/academy/lesson/barbarians-history-invasions.html#:~:text=The%20term%20%22barbarian%22%20was%20used,downfall%20of%20the%20Roman%20Empire

Beard, M. (2018, October 7). *The collaborative and inclusive nature of the Roman Empire.* History Hit. https://www.historyhit.com/the-collaborative-and-inclusive-nature-of-the-roman-empire/

Becker, J. (n.d.). *Pompeii: House of the Vettii.* Smart History. https://smarthistory.org/pompeii-house-of-the-vettii/

Bellomo, M. (2022, June 12). *Dictator: The evolution of the Roman dictatorship.* BMCR. https://bmcr.brynmawr.edu/2022/2022.06.12/

Bennett, S. (n.d.). *The Iron Age.* Khan Academy. https://www.khanacademy.org/humanities/wh

p-origins/era-3-cities-societies-and-empires-
6000-bce-to-700-c-e/32-long-distance-trade-
betaa/a/read-the-iron-age-beta
Bileta, V. (2023, February 15). *What was the crisis
    of the Third Century?* The Collector.
    https://www.thecollector.com/what-was-the-
    crisis-of-the-third-century/
Bileta, V. (2023, February 20). *What was the
    Roman legion?* The Collector.
    https://www.thecollector.com/what-was-the-
    roman-legion/
Boissoneault, L. (2017, November 16). *Before the
    fall of the Roman Republic, income inequality
    and xenophobia threatened its foundations.*
    Smithsonian Magazine.
    https://www.smithsonianmag.com/history/fall-
    roman-republic-income-inequality-and-
    xenophobia-threatened-its-foundations-
    180967249/
Burks, A. M. (2008). *Roman Slavery: A Study of
    Roman Society and Its Dependence on slaves.*
    East Tennessee State University. Retrieved from
    https://dc.etsu.edu/cgi/viewcontent.cgi?article
    =3303&context=etd
Burns, R. (2022, May 19). *Cincinnatus: A Roman
    dictator's resounding impact.* Discentes.
    https://web.sas.upenn.edu/discentes/2022/05/
    19/cincinnatus-a-roman-dictators-resounding-
    impact/
Burns, R. (2023, November 21). *First Triumvirate |
    Definition, history and significance.* Study.com.
    https://study.com/learn/lesson/julius-caesar-
    the-first-
    triumvirate.html#:~:text=The%20First%20Triu
    mvirate%20accomplished%20many,build%20hi
    s%20army%20in%20Gaul
Caesar's civil war: Ancient Rome destroys itself.
    (n.d.). History Skills.

https://www.historyskills.com/classroom/ancient-history/anc-caesar-civil-war-reading/

Calvo, J. (2022, June 6). *La importancia de la inflación en la caída del Imperio romano.* El Economista. https://www.eleconomista.es/podcasts/noticias/11801055/06/22/La-importancia-de-la-inflacion-en-la-caida-del-Imperio-romano.html

Campbell, C.J. (2022, March 30). *Peace and prosperity: What was the Pax Romana?* The Collector. https://www.thecollector.com/what-was-pax-romana/

Carr, K. (2017, September 3). *Stone Age Italy – the history of Italy.* Quatr.us. https://quatr.us/history/stone-age-italy-history-italy.htm

Cartwright, M. (2017, September 1). Roman art. In *World History Encyclopedia.* https://www.worldhistory.org/Roman_Art/

Cartwright, M. (2018, April 12). Trade in the Roman world. In *World History Encyclopedia.* https://www.worldhistory.org/article/638/trade-in-the-roman-world/

Chaliakopoulos, A. (2022, January 12). *Antiochus III the Great: The Seleucid king who took on Rome.* The Collector. https://www.thecollector.com/antiochus-iii-the-great-seleucid-king/

Chronology - Prehistory in Italy. (n.d.). Preistoria in Italia. https://www.preistoriainitalia.it/en/cronologia/

Comunale, J. (2023, November 21). *Etruscan religion, culture and influence.* Study.com. https://study.com/learn/lesson/etruscans-religion-culture.html

Crises of the Republic. (n.d.). Lumen Learning. https://courses.lumenlearning.com/atd-herkimer-westerncivilization/chapter/crises-of-the-republic/

Crises of the Roman Empire. (n.d.). Lumen Learning. https://courses.lumenlearning.com/atd-herkimer-westerncivilization/chapter/crises-of-the-roman-empire/#:~:text=Overview,%2C%20plague%2C%20and%20economic%20depression

Curiate Assembly (comitia curiata). (n.d.). Academic Dictionaries and Encyclopedias. https://en-academic.com/dic.nsf/enwiki/931745

David, J.L. (2013, March 25). The intervention of the Sabine women. In *World History Encyclopedia.* https://www.worldhistory.org/image/1125/the-intervention-of-the-sabine-women/#:~:text=by%20Jacques%2DLouis%20David&text=Fearing%20the%20emergence%20of%20a,the%20festival%20among%20Rome%27s%20neighbours

Did Christianity cause the fall of Rome? (n.d.). World Atlas. https://www.worldatlas.com/did-christianity-cause-the-fall-of-rome.html

Did stoicism have any influence on Ancient Rome? (n.d.). Stoic Simple. https://www.stoicsimple.com/did-stoicism-have-any-influence-on-ancient-rome/

Diocletian and the tetrarchy. (n.d.). Lumen Learning. https://courses.lumenlearning.com/atd-herkimer-westerncivilization/chapter/diocletian-and-the-tetrarchy/

Dyck, L.H. (n.d.). *The Gallic Wars: To northern Gaul.* Warfare History Network.

https://warfarehistorynetwork.com/the-gallic-wars-to-northern-gaul/

Etruscans: civilization, history and influence on Rome. (n.d.). TimeMaps. https://timemaps.com/civilizations/etruscans/

Ferguson, J. & Balsdon, J. (n.d.). Cicero. In *Encyclopedia Britannica.* Retrieved November 25, 2023, from https://www.britannica.com/biography/Cicero

Ferguson, J., Forsythe, G.E., Petit, P., Saller, R.P., Badian, E., MacMullen, R., Vermeule, E.D., Grummond, N., Hornblower, S., & Salmon, E.T. (n.d.). Ancient Rome. In *Encyclopedia Britannica.* Retrieved November 9, 2023, from https://www.britannica.com/place/ancient-Rome

Fernandes, F. (2022, March 14). *How to establish an empire: The Emperor Augustus transforms Rome.* The Collector. https://www.thecollector.com/augustus-transforms-rome-empire/

Frye, D. (2007, March 5). *Rome's Barbarian mercenaries.* Historynet. https://www.historynet.com/romes-barbarian-mercenaries/

Fuhrmann, C. (2011, December). *"I brought peace to the provinces": Augustus and the Rhetoric of Imperial Peace.* doi.org/10.1093/acprof:oso/9780199737840.003.0004

Garcia, B. (2018, April 18). Romulus and Remus. In *World History Encyclopedia.* https://www.worldhistory.org/Romulus_and_Remus/

Gazioğlu, H.H. (n.d.). *The "barbarization" of the Roman army.* Academia.edu. https://www.academia.edu/36861074/_THE_BARBARIZATION_OF_THE_ROMAN_ARMY

Gill, N.S. (2019, February 17). *Who were the early kings of Rome?* ThoughtCo. https://www.thoughtco.com/the-early-kings-of-rome-119374

Gill, N.S. (2019, July 1). *Economic reasons for the fall of Rome.* ThoughtCo. https://www.thoughtco.com/economic-reasons-for-fall-of-rome-118357

Gill, N.S. (2021, February 16). *Who were the Gracchi brothers of ancient Rome?* ThoughtCo. thoughtco.com/gracchi-brothers-tiberius-gaius-gracchus-112494.

Grant, M. (n.d.). Horace. In *Encyclopedia Britannica.* Retrieved November 27, 2023, from https://www.britannica.com/biography/Horace-Roman-poet

Harding, S.B. (n.d.). *City of the Seven Hills.* Heritage History. https://www.heritage-history.com/index.php?c=read&author=harding&book=seven&story=fabii

Hellie, R. (n.d.). Slavery. In *Encyclopedia Britannica.* Retrieved November 21, 2023, from https://www.britannica.com/topic/slavery-sociology

Henderson, M.M. (1968). Tiberius Gracchus and the failure of the Roman republic. *Theoria: A Journal of Social and Political Theory, 31,* 51–64. http://www.jstor.org/stable/41801828

History.com Editors. (2023, June 16). *Constantinople.* History.com. https://www.history.com/topics/middle-east/constantinople

Hoffmann, J. (n.d.). Appius Claudius Caecus. Encyclopedia.com. https://www.encyclopedia.com/science/encyclopedias-almanacs-transcripts-and-maps/appius-claudius-caecus

How did the Etruscans shape Roman history and society. (n.d.). DailyHistory.org. https://www.dailyhistory.org/How_did_the_Et ruscans_shape_Roman_history_and_society

How the First Triumvirate changed ancient Rome. (n.d.). History Skills. https://www.historyskills.com/classroom/ancie nt-history/anc-1st-triumvirate-reading/

Ides of March: The Death of Caesar. (n.d.). Penelope.uchicago.edu. https://penelope.uchicago.edu/~grout/encyclo paedia_romana/calendar/ides.html

Jarus, O. (2022, September 2). *Attila the Hun: Biography of the 'Scourge of God.'* Live Science. https://www.livescience.com/44417-attila-the-hun.html

Jasiński, J. (2019, February 18). *I found Rome a city of bricks and left it a city of marble.* Imperium Romanum. https://imperiumromanum.pl/en/curiosities/i-found-rome-a-city-of-bricks-and-left-it-a-city-of-marble/

Jasiński, J. (2020, April 18). *Values professed by Romans.* Imperium Romanum. https://imperiumromanum.pl/en/curiosities/v alues-professed-by-romans/#:~:text=Values%20%E2%80%8B%E2 %80%8Bfor%20the,%2C%20meaning%20%E2 %80%9Chusband%E2%80%9D

Kamash, Z. Shipley, L., Galaakis, Y. & Skaltsa, S. (2013). *Iron Age and Roman Italy.* In World Archeology at the Pitts Rivers Museum: A Characterization. Archaeopress, p. 336-357. http://archaeopress.com/Public/download.asp? id=%7B30DA1356-8CE5-467F-AD80-B67B30B82EA6%7D#:~:text=16.4%20Iron%20 Age%20Italy&text=The%20Etruscan%20Iron% 20Age%20material,and%20ceramics%20(43%2 0examples)

Kenney, E.J. (n.d.). Ovid. In *Encyclopedia Britannica*. Retrieved January 1, 2024, from https://www.britannica.com/biography/Ovid-Roman-poet

Kershaw, D. (2023, August 29). *The Twelve Tables: The foundation of Roman law*. History Cooperative. https://historycooperative.org/the-twelve-tables/

Kessler, P. & Dawson, E. (2019, January 11). *Iron Age Italy 800-400 BC*. The History Files. https://www.historyfiles.co.uk/FeaturesEurope/ItalyIronAge01.htm

Kessler, P. (n.d.). *Early Italy (Iron Age)*. The History Files. https://www.historyfiles.co.uk/KingListsEurope/ItalyCulturesIronAge.htm

Kinder, H. & Hilgemann, W. (1996). World Historic Atlas. ISTMO

Kindy, D. (2021, September 29). *Where did the ancient Etruscans come from?* Smithsonian Magazine. https://www.smithsonianmag.com/smart-news/dna-analysis-shows-early-etruscans-were-homegrown-180978772/#:~:text=Before%20the%20glory%20of%20Rome,the%20known%20world%20for%20centuries

Kingdoms of the Germanic Tribes - Scirii. (n.d.). The History Files. https://www.historyfiles.co.uk/KingListsEurope/BarbarianScirii.htm

Lakha, S. (n.d.). *Overcoming ancient history challenges- Common problems and solutions*. Spires.co. https://spires.co/online-ancient-history-tutors/undergraduate/overcoming-ancient-history-challenges-common-problems-and-solutions

Latins. (n.d.). Oxford Reference. https://www.oxfordreference.com/display/10.1093/oi/authority.20110803100053207

Lecture 26: Fall of the Roman Republic, 133-27 BC. (n.d.). web.ics.purdue.edu. https://web.ics.purdue.edu/~rauhn/fall_of_republic.htm#:~:text=Internal%20turmoil%20provoked%20in%20133,Republic%2C%20133%2D27%20BC

Lendering, J. (2019, April 26). *Second Triumvirate.* Livius.org. https://www.livius.org/articles/concept/triumvir/second-triumvirate/

Lesso, R. (2022, July 1). *What Are the Origins of Stoicism?* The Collector. https://www.thecollector.com/what-are-the-origins-of-stoicism-history/

Lloyd, J. (2013, April 30). Roman army. In *World History Encyclopedia.* https://www.worldhistory.org/Roman_Army/

Malvasi, M. (2023, October 15). *A message from Rome.* The Imaginative Conservative. https://theimaginativeconservative.org/2023/10/message-rome-mark-malvasi.html

Mandal, D. (2023, June 19). *25 Incredible ancient Roman quotes you should know.* Realm of History. https://www.realmofhistory.com/2023/06/19/25-ancient-roman-quotes/

Marcus Tullius Cicero. (n.d.). In times of war. Goodreads. https://www.goodreads.com/quotes/49233-in-times-of-war-the-law-falls-silent-silent-enim

Mark, J. (2014, September 20). Odoacer. In *World History Encyclopedia.* https://www.worldhistory.org/Odoacer/

Mark, J. (2017, November 9). The crisis of the Third Century. In *World History Encyclopedia.*

https://www.worldhistory.org/Crisis_of_the_T
hird_Century/

McDonald, A.H. (n.d.). Tacitus. In Encyclopedia
Britannica. Retrieved December 1, 2023, from
https://www.britannica.com/biography/Tacitus
-Roman-historian

Menenius. (n.d.). Heritage History.
https://www.heritage-
history.com/index.php?c=resources&s=char-
dir&f=menenius

Montoya, R. (2022, May 3). *The 30 most important
Roman structures that you can visit today.* The
Tour Guy. https://thetourguy.com/travel-
blog/italy/rome/most-important-roman-
structures-that-you-can-visit-today/

Nuragic monuments of Sardinia. (n.d.). UNESCO
World Heritage Centre.
https://whc.unesco.org/en/tentativelists/6557/
#:~:text=Nuragic%20cultural%20heritage%20o
f%20Bronze,extra%20classic%20constructions
%20of%20any

Odoacer and the Fall of Rome. (n.d.). Lumen
Learning.
https://courses.lumenlearning.com/atd-
herkimer-westerncivilization/chapter/odoacer-
and-the-fall-of-rome/

Ogilvie, Robert Maxwell. "Livy". Encyclopedia
Britannica, 1 Jan. 2023,
https://www.britannica.com/biography/Livy.
Accessed 6 December 2023.

Phelan, J. (2022, September 25). *Why did the
Roman Empire split in two?* Live Science.
https://www.livescience.com/why-roman-
empire-split-in-two

Rocess, G. (2019, November 12). *History is filled
with the sound of silken slippers.* Medium.com.
https://glennrocess.medium.com/history-is-
filled-with-the-sound-of-silken-slippers-going-

downstairs-and-wooden-shoes-coming-up-a3bf57f544f3

Roman culture and the Aeneid. (n.d.). Faculty.gvsu.edu. https://faculty.gvsu.edu/websterm/Aeneid.htm

Roman Emperors during Pax Romana: 27BC to 180AD timeline. (n.d.). Timetoast. https://www.timetoast.com/timelines/roman-emperors-during-pax-romana-27bc-to-180ad

Roman Empire politics | Political reasons for the fall of Rome. (n.d.). Ancient Rome. https://mariamilani.com/ancient_rome/political-aspects-in-the-fall-of-the-roman-empire.htm

Roman Republic. (2023, October 19). National Geographic Society. https://education.nationalgeographic.org/resource/roman-republic/

Rome Geography. (n.d.). History Histories. http://www.historyshistories.com/rome-geography.html

Romulus and Remus: Story of the Founding of Rome. (2016, March 24). Retrieved from https://study.com/academy/lesson/romulus-and-remus-story-of-the-founding-of-rome.html.

Sal. (2020, November 14). *The rape of the Sabine women.* Medium.com. https://medium.com/lessons-from-history/the-rape-of-the-sabine-women-907950335319

Saunders, J.L. (n.d.). Stoicism. In *Encyclopedia Britannica.* Retrieved November 9, 2023, from https://www.britannica.com/topic/Stoicism

Schultz, C. E., Ward, A. M., Heichelheim, F. M., & Yeo, C. A. (2019). Early Roman Society, Religion, and Values. In *A History of the Roman People* (7th ed.). Routledge. Retrieved from https://pressbooks.claremont.edu/clas112pomonavalentine/chapter/94/

Servile Wars. (n.d.). Heritage History. https://www.heritage-history.com/index.php?c=resources&s=war-dir&f=wars_servile

Shaw, G. (2015, March 27). *Stone-age Italians defleshed their dead*. Science. https://www.science.org/content/article/stone-age-italians-defleshed-their-dead

Stanfield, J. (2023, October 19). *Julius Caesar*. National Geographic. https://education.nationalgeographic.org/resource/julius-caesar/

Sterling, D. (n.d.). *Julius Caesar versus Pompey: A civil war of subterfuge*. Warfare History Network. https://warfarehistorynetwork.com/julius-caesar-vs-pompey-a-civil-war-of-subterfuge/

Taylor, L. (n.d.). *The Etruscans, an introduction*. Khan Academy. https://www.khanacademy.org/humanities/ap-art-history/ancient-mediterranean-ap/ap-ancient-etruria/a/the-etruscans-an-introduction

Teach democracy. (n.d.). Constitutional Rights Foundation. https://www.crf-usa.org/bill-of-rights-in-action/bria-23-3-b-cicero-defender-of-the-roman-republic

The Cursus Publicus: The courier service of the Roman Empire. (n.d.). History of Information. https://www.historyofinformation.com/detail.php?id=1394

The Editors of Encyclopedia Britannica. (n.d.). Appius Claudius Caecus. In *Encyclopedia Britannica*. Retrieved January 2, 2024, from https://www.britannica.com/biography/Appius-Claudius-Caecus

The Editors of Encyclopedia Britannica. (n.d.). Barbarian. In *Encyclopedia Britannica*. Retrieved January 4, 2024, from https://www.britannica.com/topic/barbarian-invasions

The Editors of Encyclopedia Britannica. (n.d.). Battle of Actium. In *Encyclopedia Britannica.* Retrieved January 4, 2024, from https://www.britannica.com/event/Battle-of-Actium-ancient-Roman-history

The Editors of Encyclopedia Britannica. (n.d.). Colosseum. In *Encyclopedia Britannica.* Retrieved January 3, 2024, from https://www.britannica.com/topic/Colosseum

The Editors of Encyclopedia Britannica. (n.d.). Five Good Emperors. In *Encyclopedia Britannica.* Retrieved January 3, 2024, from https://www.britannica.com/topic/Five-Good-Emperors

The Editors of Encyclopedia Britannica. (n.d.). Gnaeus Marcius Coriolanus. In *Encyclopedia Britannica.* Retrieved January 2, 2024, from https://www.britannica.com/topic/Gnaeus-Marcius-Coriolanus

The Editors of Encyclopedia Britannica. (n.d.). Latifundium. In *Encyclopedia Britannica.* Retrieved January 2, 2024, from https://www.britannica.com/topic/latifundium

The Editors of Encyclopedia Britannica. (n.d.). Latin League. In *Encyclopedia Britannica.* Retrieved January 2, 2024, from https://www.britannica.com/topic/Latin-League

The Editors of Encyclopedia Britannica. (n.d.). Lucius Cornelius Cinna. In *Encyclopedia Britannica.* Retrieved January 2, 2024, from https://www.britannica.com/biography/Lucius-Cornelius-Cinna

The Editors of Encyclopedia Britannica. (n.d.). Macedonian wars. In *Encyclopedia Britannica.* Retrieved January 2, 2024, from https://www.britannica.com/event/Macedonia n-Wars

The Editors of Encyclopedia Britannica. (n.d.). Odoacer. In *Encyclopedia Britannica*. Retrieved January 2, 2024, from https://www.britannica.com/biography/Odoace r

The Editors of Encyclopedia Britannica. (n.d.). Pompey the Great. In *Encyclopedia Britannica*. Retrieved January 2, 2024, from https://www.britannica.com/biography/Pompe y-the-Great

The Editors of Encyclopedia Britannica. (n.d.). Province. In *Encyclopedia Britannica*. Retrieved January 2, 2024, from https://www.britannica.com/topic/province-ancient-Roman-government

The Editors of Encyclopedia Britannica. (n.d.). Punic Wars summary. In *Encyclopedia Britannica*. Retrieved January 2, 2024, from https://www.britannica.com/summary/Punic-Wars

The Editors of Encyclopedia Britannica. (n.d.). Punic Wars. In *Encyclopedia Britannica*. Retrieved January 2, 2024, from https://www.britannica.com/event/Punic-Wars/Campaigns-in-Sicily-and-Spain

The Editors of Encyclopedia Britannica. (n.d.). Roman Empire. In *Encyclopedia Britannica*. Retrieved January 3, 2024, from https://www.britannica.com/place/Roman-Empire

The Editors of Encyclopedia Britannica. (n.d.). Roman Republic. In *Encyclopedia Britannica*. Retrieved January 2, 2024, from https://www.britannica.com/place/Roman-Republic

The Editors of Encyclopedia Britannica. (n.d.). Romulus and Remus. In *Encyclopedia Britannica*. Retrieved January 2, 2024, from https://www.britannica.com/biography/Romulus-and-Remus

The Editors of Encyclopedia Britannica. (n.d.). Sabine. In *Encyclopedia Britannica*. Retrieved January 2, 2024, from https://www.britannica.com/topic/Sabine

The Editors of Encyclopedia Britannica. (n.d.). Senate. In *Encyclopedia Britannica*. Retrieved January 2, 2024, from https://www.britannica.com/topic/Senate-Roman-history

The Editors of Encyclopedia Britannica. (n.d.). Social wars. In *Encyclopedia Britannica*. Retrieved January 2, 2024, from https://www.britannica.com/event/Social-War-Roman-history

The Editors of Encyclopedia Britannica. (n.d.). Tanaquil. In *Encyclopedia Britannica*. Retrieved January 2, 2024, from https://www.britannica.com/biography/Tanaquil

The Editors of Encyclopedia Britannica. (n.d.). Titus Tatius. In *Encyclopedia Britannica*. Retrieved January 2, 2024, from https://www.britannica.com/topic/Titus-Tatius

The fall of Rome. (n.d.). Students of History. https://www.studentsofhistory.com/the-fall-of-rome#:~:text=Many%20of%20the%20issues%20that,poor%20struggled%20to%20find%20work

The geography of ancient Rome. (n.d.). Students of History. https://www.studentsofhistory.com/geography-of-the-roman-world

The Italian Bronze Age. (n.d.). Encyclopedia.com. https://www.encyclopedia.com/humanities/enc

yclopedias-almanacs-transcripts-and-
maps/italian-bronze-age

The Punic Wars versus Carthage. (n.d.). Students of
History.
https://www.studentsofhistory.com/the-punic-
wars#:~:text=The%20Third%20Punic%20War
%20was,going%20to%20war%20with%20Numi
dia

The Roman Empire: A Brief History. (n.d.).
Milwaukee Public Museum.
https://www.mpm.edu/research-
collections/anthropology/anthropology-
collections-research/mediterranean-oil-
lamps/roman-empire-brief-
history#:~:text=The%20history%20of%20the%
20Roman,31%20BC%20%E2%80%93%20AD%
20476

The Roman kingdom (753–509 BC). (n.d.). Digital
Maps of the Ancient World.
https://digitalmapsoftheancientworld.com/anci
ent-history/history-ancient-rome/the-roman-
kingdom-753-509-
bc/#:~:text=Also%20referred%20to%20as%20t
he,Palatine%20hill%20in%20753%20BC

The Sabines: A glimpse into an ancient Italic tribe.
(2023, March 19). Weird Italy.
https://weirditaly.com/2023/03/19/the-
sabines-a-glimpse-into-an-ancient-italic-tribe/

The Second Triumvirate: The ruthless alliance that
finally brought the Roman Republic to its end.
(n.d.). History Skills.
https://www.historyskills.com/classroom/ancie
nt-history/second-triumvirate-reading/

The Seven Kings. (n.d.). Lumen Learning.
https://courses.lumenlearning.com/atd-
herkimer-westerncivilization/chapter/the-
seven-kings/

The Shift East. (n.d.). Lumen Learning. https://courses.lumenlearning.com/atd-herkimer-westerncivilization/chapter/the-shift-east/

The Struggle of the Orders: Plebeians and patricians. (2016, November 2). Retrieved from https://study.com/academy/lesson/the-struggle-of-the-orders-plebeians-and-patricians.html.

The Struggle of the Orders: Plebeians unite to lift their shackles. (n.d.). Sites.psu.edu. https://sites.psu.edu/struggleoftheorders/

Traces of Ancient Rome in the Modern World. (n.d.). National Geographic. https://education.nationalgeographic.org/resource/traces-ancient-rome-modern-world/

Valgiglio, E. (n.d.). Sulla. In *Encyclopedia Britannica.* Retrieved December 14, 2023, from https://www.britannica.com/biography/Sulla

Vandiver, T. (n.d.). *Revelations of Rome in Virgil's Aeneid.* https://hilo.hawaii.edu/campuscenter/hohonu/volumes/documents/Vol06x16RevelationsofRomeinVirgilsAeneid.pdf

Vermeulen, M. (2020, August 1). *The Roman Senate: An in-depth understanding.* The Collector. https://www.thecollector.com/roman-senate/

Vernon, J. (2023, March 14). *The Ides of March—a day of murder that forever changed history.* National Geographic. https://www.nationalgeographic.com/history/article/julius-caesar-ides-of-march

Virginia. (n.d.). Heritage History. https://www.heritage-history.com/index.php?c=resources&s=char-dir&f=virginia

Vuckovic, A. (2023, June 25). *Numa Pompilius: The legendary second king of Rome.* Ancient

Origins. https://www.ancient-origins.net/history-famous-people/numa-pompilius-0018697

Vulic, V. (2023, June 10). *Roman Empire map: Unveiling its vast territory*. The Roman Empire. https://roman-empire.net/maps/map-of-ancient-rome/

Vulic, V. (2023, November 27). *Uncovering the causes and legacy of the fall of Rome*. The Roman Empire. https://roman-empire.net/decline/uncovering-the-causes-and-legacy-of-the-fall-of-rome/

Wasson, D. (2016, April 18). Second Triumvirate. In *World History Encyclopedia*. https://www.worldhistory.org/Second_Triumvirate/

Whelan, E. (2020, July 8). *Romulus and Remus: Murder and the foundation of Rome*. Classical Wisdom. https://classicalwisdom.com/mythology/romulus-and-remus-murder-and-the-foundation-of-rome/

White, A. (2011). *The role of Marius's military reforms in the decline of the Roman Republic*. https://wou.edu/history/files/2015/08/andrewwhite.pdf

Williams, R. (2022, December 11). *The Sicilian slave revolts of ancient Rome*. Medium.com. https://medium.com/lessons-from-history/the-sicilian-slave-revolts-of-ancient-rome-22196981315e

Winters, R. (2019, January 14). *The seven kings of Rome: Tumultuous origins of the Roman Republic*. Ancient Origins. https://www.ancient-origins.net/history-famous-people/seven-kings-rome-tumultuous-origins-roman-republic-008821#google_vignette

Zhou, W. (2015). *The Roman Army: Strategy, Tactics, and Innovation.* Young Historians Conference. Portland State University. https://pdxscholar.library.pdx.edu/cgi/viewcon tent.cgi?referer=&httpsredir=1&article=1075&c ontext=younghistorians

Image References

Barskefranck. (2019, August 28). *Roman arena antique Coliseum.* [Image]. Pixabay. https://pixabay.com/photos/roman-arena-antique-coliseum-4436335/

Carlos Felipe Ramírez Mesa. (2022, September 10). *A statue of a bear and several baby bears.* [Image]. Unsplash. https://unsplash.com/photos/a-statue-of-a-bear-and-several-baby-bears-WwujhyrZH30

Dozemode. (2019, March 27). *Roman chariot race Rome Colloseum.* [Image]. Pixabay. https://pixabay.com/photos/-4086569/

Efrye. (2015, February 7). *Julius Caesar statue Italy.* [Image]. Pixabay. https://pixabay.com/photos/julius-caesar-caesar-statue-italy-626422/

Eugenio Barboza. (2020, November 4). *Art, Italy, statue.* [Image]. Pexels. https://www.pexels.com/es-es/foto/arte-italia-estatua-escultura-5793604/

Fabio Fistarol. (2021, January 13). *Aerial view of city buildings during daytime.* [Image]. Unsplash. https://unsplash.com/photos/aerial-view-of-city-buildings-during-daytime-t6BTXRe5BRc

Gioia Maurizi. (2022, February 26). *A very tall building with lots of columns.* [Image]. Unsplash. https://unsplash.com/photos/a-very-tall-building-with-lots-of-columns-4jQRmAUiffY

Gioele Fazzeri. (2021, April 30). *Man in gray and black suit holding brown wooden stick.* [Image]. Unsplash. https://unsplash.com/photos/man-in-gray-and-black-suit-holding-brown-wooden-stick-VPrcvxP9aUw

Ha110k. (2019, November 2). *Horse soldier warrior war battle.* [Image]. Pixabay. https://pixabay.com/photos/horse-soldier-warrior-war-battle-4596827/

JOE Planas. (2022, March 14). *A tall white tower with a clock on top of it.* [Image]. Unsplash. https://unsplash.com/photos/a-tall-white-tower-with-a-clock-on-top-of-it-kDiYOROr8vU

Maria Teneva. (2023, December 14). *A path going up a hill on a foggy day.* [Image] Unsplash. https://unsplash.com/photos/a-path-going-up-a-hill-on-a-foggy-day-TfeJqoie5dQ

Marina Gr. (2021, October 7). *Art architecture statue.* [Image]. Pexels. https://www.pexels.com/es-es/foto/arte-arquitectura-estatua-al-aire-libre-9818108/

Matteo del Piano. (2023, March 16). *The ruins of a Roman city lit up at night.* [Image]. Unsplash. https://unsplash.com/photos/the-ruins-of-a-roman-city-lit-up-at-night-Lfo7YMVHYA8

Photos_Marta. (2018, April 6). *Coins Roman coins money.* [Image]. Pixabay. https://pixabay.com/photos/-3298260/

PublicDomainPictures. (2012, February 27). *Ancient Roman Empire armor Caesar.* [Image]. Pixabay. https://pixabay.com/photos/ancient-roman-empire-armor-caesar-18496/

Richardprins. (2011). *Map of ancient Rome, showing the Servian wall with a blue line, and the Aurelian wall with a red line. Highlands are shown in pink (including the Seven Hills of Rome, with names) and lowlands are shown in white.* [Map]. Retrieved from https://commons.wikimedia.org/wiki/File:Map_of_ancient_Rome.svg

Ridoe. (2017, July 11). *Pont-Du-Gard Nimes.* [Image]. Pixabay. https://pixabay.com/photos/pont-du-gard-nimes-arles-ales-2493762/

Stephanie Klepacki. (2023, May 12). *A statue of a woman in a park.* [Image]. Unsplash. https://unsplash.com/photos/a-statue-of-a-woman-in-a-park-J7Jn2Vn1Xjs

Sweetaholic. (2020, January 23). *Hadrians' Wall Roman wall.* [Image]. Pixabay. https://pixabay.com/photos/hadrians-wall-roman-wall-4788570/

The_Double_A. (2017, January 31). *Colosseum Rome city Roman Coliseum.* [Image]. Pixabay. https://pixabay.com/photos/-2030643/

Travelspot. (2015, April 3). *Italy necropolis Etruscan dig.* [Image]. Pixabay. https://pixabay.com/photos/italy-necropolis-etruscan-dig-704870/

Made in the USA
Monee, IL
29 March 2024

12076439-bb07 408e-809d-f15e03aba041R01